Forth to the Sea

By
William Fyfe Hendrie

This book is dedicated to my aunts and uncles,

Andrew,
Bessie,
Douglas and Nan,
John and Maude,
Mabel,
Matt and Betty,
Tom and Johan,
and my great aunts
Christina
and Mary,

all of whose help and encouragement, I value greatly.

"Forth to the Sea" first printed and published June, 1980.

ISBN 0 9507156 0 3

Also by the same author *"Bo'ness, Three Hundred Years"*
"West Lothian Lore"
and with James McCue *"Alice in Wonderland"* a dramatised version of Lewis Carroll's famous children's classic, published by McMillan Education Ltd.

Acknowledgements
Cover and illustrations—Guthrie Pollock
Photographs—John Doherty
Proofs—Charles Grant

My thanks to the Editor of *"The Edinburgh Evening News"* and *"Scotland's Magazine"* for permission to include material which originally appeared in these publications.

Printed by S.K.I. Graphics (Scotland) Ltd., 45 St Marnock Street, Bridgeton, Glasgow.

Contents

Loch Ard and Ben Lomond (3,192 feet)

The River Forth rises on the slopes of Ben Lomond high above the shores of Loch Ard. From there it flows below the first of the Forth bridges at Aberfoyle and on to Stirling, and Alloa where it becomes tidal.

Forth Bridge, Aberfoyle

Chapter 1

From Alloa To Airth

"A merchant of Alloa may trade to all parts of the world." So wrote the author of "Robinson Crusoe," Daniel Defoe, when he visited Alloa, the county town of Clackmannanshire, which, as schoolchildren used to learn, is "Scotland's smallest county with the largest name."

Looking at Alloa's now derelict harbour area it is hard to imagine that in Defoe's day more than 100 sailing ships were registered there and that it is less than 15 years since the port of Alloa was officially closed by the British Transport Commission.

Despite the ruins of an old pub still bearing the name of the "Old Ship Inn" and a fishing boat anchored in the river, Alloa harbour, with its view of flat green fields, seems far too far inland ever to have been the home of sea-going ships, but it was in fact its position far up the Forth, right in the heart of Central Scotland, which in the eighteenth century gave Alloa its original advantage.

For in those days Scotland's roads scarcely justified the name, being but muddy quagmires in winter and rutted dust bowls in summer, and so the farther inland that cargoes could be transported by water the better.

The middle of the eighteenth century was the time when the merchants of Glasgow were making their fortune, importing large quantities of tobacco from the American colonies. Most of the tobacco was imported through the Clyde, but much of the profit in this trade came from the re-export of the tobacco to Holland and the other countries of Europe, who could not buy direct from the British colonies because of the Navigation Laws. The Glasgow tobacco lords were quick to spot the advantages of Alloa as the nearest east coast port to their city.

Packhorse trains carried bales of tobacco overland from the Clyde to Alloa, where some of it was manufactured into cigars and snuff, but most was loaded on to sailing ships in the harbour and carried to the Low Countries where the Dutch preferred to process it themselves.

From 1783 onwards, the Dutch cigar makers could buy direct from American growers, for the War of Independence had set the colonies free, and the Glasgow tobacco barons and Alloa lost this part of their trade. Alloa's old links with Glasgow received an even worse blow in 1790 when Scotland's first canal — the 351mile-long Forth and Clyde Canal — provided the city with a direct water link with the new port of Grangemouth, which rapidly grew up where the canal entered the Forth.

Despite these setbacks, Alloa remained busy dealing with cargoes of grain and sand for the town's breweries and glassworks, industries which still thrive in Alloa long after the harbour has been forgotten.

Beer and bottles has been a happy partnership for many years, but with the increasing use of cans it is a happy situation for Alloa that its glassworks make many other kinds of containers, a range which is attractively displayed in the windows of the United Glassworks only a short distance away from the old harbour.

The import of pit props for the area's coal mines steadily increased. It was decided in 1861 to build a large new dock basin, and when it was completed two years later it was 450 feet long, 137 feet broad and 24 feet deep and had a 50 feet wide entrance gate. At this time a dry dock for ship repairing was also constructed and there was also a shipbuilding yard in the town.

The port was active until the 1930s when Kincardine Road Bridge was opened. The bridge was designed with a central swing span, which opens to allow vessels upstream, but despite this, the bridge was the main reason for Alloa's decline. For it so greatly improved road communication between the town and Grangemouth that it became faster for ships to discharge at Grangemouth and for their cargoes to be carried by road to Alloa's factories than for the vessels to navigate the shallows to the town's own dock.

The Second World War brought a temporary boost to Alloa with the building of many small naval vessels, and after 1945 attempts were made to modernise the port, including the electrification of the dock gates, but apart from specialist cargoes it could not compete with Grangemouth.

At the beginning of the 1960s the British Transport Commission officially closed Alloa to navigation. Now the old dock has been filled in and this area of flat land is being offered for industrial development.

It is interesting to note that its immediate access to water transport, Alloa's original advantage, is stressed as one of the main selling points.

And so it is possible that a new chapter could be written in Alloa's history.

Across the river from Alloa lies South Alloa where Globe Petroleum still have a jetty. However the occasional arrival of a small coastal tanker is in marked contrast to the days a century ago, when South Alloa, was a bustling port with a direct rail link to Glasgow.

South Alloa's main import was Scandinavian pit props for the collieries of Central Scotland and it is said that on a warm sunny summer day visitors smelt South Alloa long before they reached it because of the sweet smelling resin oozing out of the timber, piled high in the prop yards.

It was the availability of timber, not imported but home grown, which in an earlier age brought fame to another of the villages on this stretch of the river, Airth, for it was there that Scotland's Royal Dockyard was established. During the sixteenth century many small wooden-hulled vessels were build there for the navy which had been founded by King James IV.

While it is strange to imagine that Scotland's naval dockyard was situated so far inland, it is even harder to believe that a naval battle was also once fought on this peaceful section of the Forth, but such was indeed the case. The battle took place during the 1745 Jacobite uprising when some of Prince Charles' followers succeeded in seizing several small cannon, which they set up overlooking the river at neighbouring Dunmore.

News of this reached Edinburgh and orders were given to a naval vessel at Leith to sail up the Forth to dislodge the rebels. This must have seemed an easy mission, but the captain and crew of the naval vessel were soon disillusioned because the Jacobites put up a stubborn resistance.

All day, the calm of the Stirlingshire countryside was shattered by the steady exchange of shots between the shore battery and the naval vessel which, in the end, was forced to sail back down river without having moved the Jacobites. On the way, however, the naval captain made certain that the rebels would not be able to seize any boats for he destroyed every vessel he found between Airth and Grangemouth.

At Dunmore, the only boats left in the "pool," as the little creek is called, are the black painted keeled dinghies with which the village men keep up the Forth's last links with its once prosperous salmon fishing.

Before the last war, salmon fishing was a full-time industry at Dunmore, but now, even during the July height of the season, which stretches from February to August, there are not even enough salmon to keep one fisherman employed. The men folk return only in the evenings and at weekends to fish the river.

Main reason for the fall in the number of salmon, according to the Dunmore men, is pollution, which, they allege, is worsened by the distilleries and breweries on the opposite bank.

As he painted his upturned boat one of the village's oldest fishermen, who can well remember the days when Dunmore salmon fetched top prices on the London market, told me angrily: "Why, I've even seen the fish leaping out of the water, when they meet the discharge of hops and yeast for both of these substances eat up all the oxygen in the water leaving none for the salmon."

The Dunmore fishermen are, however, hopeful that salmon fishing may soon improve for the Forth Conservancy Board is increasingly

Horseshoe Door of the Old Smiddy, Dunmore

strict about the discharge of effluent into the river and the breweries, distilleries and other industries are doing their utmost to comply with the rules, while the completion of Alloa's new sewage purification plant should also help to reduce the pollution.

While salmon fishing from Dunmore continues, at least on a small scale, the other industry for which the little village was once famous, the making of pottery, has long since ceased. Dunmore pottery was famed for its fineness and its attractive brown glaze. Any pieces which survive in the village houses are today considered family heirlooms, carefully handed down from generation to generation.

Unlike the pottery, the village blacksmith's shop still stands and although it is now almost 20 years since horses came there to be shod, it still attracts a lot of attention from visitors because of its entrance, which is shaped like a horseshoe.

Apart from the smithy there is much to look at in Dunmore for it was one of Scotland's first "model" villages, carefully planned and built during Victorian times by Catherine, Countess of Dunmore, to provide what were by the standard of those days ideal living conditions for her estate workers and their families.

Countess Catherine spent much of her life south of the Border and thus it was that the Scottish workers of Dunmore came to find themselves living in a distinctly English-style hamlet, complete with diamond-paned lattice-windowed cottages set neatly round a village green.

But, while the Anglicised tastes of the Countess influenced the style of building at Dunmore, they could not affect the villagers' choice of sport and so, instead of cricket on the village green, it has always been bowls which have been played there. This is still the case today.

Whether or not Countess Catherine approved of her estate workers choice of sport is not recorded, but she did thoughtfully provide for any who in the course of play might work up a thirst, by providing a drinking fountain. The fountain, which was brought all the way from London, still stands in the middle of the green, but today it fails to live up to the message inscribed upon it:

"Here quench your thirst and mark in me, an emblem of true charity.
Who while my bounty I restore, am neither heard or seen to flow.
Repaid by fresh supplies from Heaven, for every cup of water given."

One feature of the village, which would not seem out of place in a giant curiosity shop, is the well known Dunmore folly. This piece of ostentatious building took the form of a giant stone pineapple built on the Countess Catherine's estate.

Why such an unusual design was chosen for this garden house at Dunmore has never been explained, but, tropical pineapples were carefully cultivated in the hothouses of some English Victorian stately homes, so possibly at one time the real fruit grew alongside the stone folly in the hothouses which flanked it on the Stirlingshire estate.

The Dunmore Pineapple Folly was recently gifted to the National Trust for Scotland and is now available to rent as a holiday cottage through the Landmark Trust.

Down stream from Dunmore the next village is Airth, already mentioned as the site of the royal dockyard. Since those proud days much land has been reclaimed and not only is there now no trace of the dockyard, but the village now finds itself situated half a mile inland, with flat green fields separating it from the river.

Only a few carved sailing ships, now anchored securely to the lintel stones of some of the houses, act as a reminder of its seafaring days.

Airth has, however, other items of historic interest, well worth turning off the Stirling to Grangemouth Low Road to inspect. For hidden behind the main street, are several attractive eighteenth-century town houses clustered around the mercat cross.

The weather-beaten stone cross, which bears the coats of arms of the two prominent local landowning families—the Elphinstones and the Bruces—was erected as long ago as 1697, but the much older original market cross of Airth can also still be found in a field at the top of the hill behing the village.

The remains of this early cross act as a reminder that the original village of Airth grew up along the crest of the hill in the shadow of the impressive castle, which still dominates the ridge and which although not open to the public can be easily seen from the main road.

Airth Castle's main claim to fame is the legend that it was there that the Scottish hero Sir William Wallace performed one of his famous feats of strength. During Wallace's time the castle fell into the hands of the English and, to make matters worse, they used it as a prison in which to keep captive the Scottish partiot's uncle.

Wallace vowed to avenge the family honour by setting free his uncle and so, with only a handful of followers, he crept across the rolling plain to the east of the castle, climbed silently up the steep hill and was so successful in his surprise attack that his band were able to storm the castle and to kill all 100 members of the English garrison.

Standing beneath the turreted battlements of the oldest surviving part of the castle, which is believed to date from the year 1408, the estate's gamekeeper, appropriately named Mr Hunter, who has stayed there all his life, proudly told me of the castle's past from the time of Fergus de Erth until it came into the possession of the Graham family.

Inside the castle, which is now a luxury hotel, I admired the beautiful balconied entrance hall and the gracefully proportioned rooms, which were added during the eighteenth century to turn this ancient fortress into a stately Georgian-style mansion house.

The long-disused graveyard, at the foot of the North Tower and the adjacent ruins of Airth's original parish church, proved fascinating to explore and it was there on a moss covered tombstone that I discovered this verse:—

"Though winds and seas full 40 years
Have tossed me to and fro,
In spite of these, by God's decrees,
I'm anchored here.below."

Thus I uncovered one last link between Airth and the sea and was also reminded that it was time to get back to the river.

During the eighteenth century the glassworks of Alloa must have been called upon to produce many whisky bottles, for only a short distance down river was situated Kilbagie Distillery, which in 1780 was claimed to be the world's largest producer of whisky.

Even in those days most of the whisky went for export, being shipped through the specially created "free port" of Kennet Pans. Kennet Pans' other main export was coal from the pits owned by the ninth Earl of Dundonald, the enlightened Scottish colliery owner, who did more than any other man to end the terrible practice of "thirldom," which entailed the buying and selling of the miners and their wives and families along with the pits in which they worked.

Having set his miners free from serfdom however, Lord Dundonald still took a great paternal interest in them, introducing a compulsory savings scheme which worked so well that he later noted that all of his men were not only able "to lay in a supply of beef for their families in November" but were also able to afford to buy "silver watches" and to have "clocks in all their houses."

It is these miners' rows at Kennet which it is now proposed to turn into a folk museum featuring the social life of the Scottish miners.

In some matters at least, it may be that we could learn from this interesting eighteenth century attempt to improve living standards, for, remembering all the recent controversy over the provision of a third of a pint of milk a day for our school-children, it is interesting to note that Lord Dundonald, almost two centuries ago in 1780, bought 13 cows to ensure that his miners' bairns would not go short.

Visitors to Clackmannan easily spot the castle or tower, which from 1365 until 1772 was the home of the Bruce family. Set high on its hill, it dominates the attractive little town, but travelling on the main road from Alloa to Kincardine it is equally easy to miss its other historic attractions: These are all tucked away up the hill from the main road, clustered round the belfry tower which is the only remaining part of Clackmannan's tolbooth, built in 1592 at the great cost of £284.

For their money the good folk of Clackmannan seem to have got a good bargain for the tolbooth housed not only the local court, but also the jailer's house and the prison. However, it needed few cells as justice in those days tended to be swifter than today, usually taking the form of capital chastisement administered with the lash at the mercat cross, on which can still be seen the marks of the chains used to hold the wrongdoers while they were whipped.

From the hill above the town it is a good idea to take heed of Clackmannanshire's motto, "Look aboot ye," for from up there it is possible to take a good look at the river to judge how it is progressing on its passage to the sea.

Left behind now are the windings which tangled its course above Alloa, looking so much like a strand of blue wool with which a kitten has been having fun, and instead it now runs fast and free for Kincardine, where the road bridge spans it just before it begins to broaden to reach all of three miles between Bo'ness and Culross.

Chapter 2

The Silver Link

The Silver Link, that was the proud nickname forged for Kincardine Bridge when it was opened by Lord Elgin on October 29th, 1936, and today, after over 40 years of uninterrupted use, it is as untarnished as ever. For, although since 1964 it has been overshadowed by the more famous Forth Road Bridge, it is still Kincardine's proud boast that it is a world record holder, while its rival down river soon lost its claim as longest suspension bridge in Europe to Lisbon's Salazar Bridge.

Kincardine's claim to fame is a swing bridge, because its 364-foot long central swing span has never been equalled and its faultless operation for more than four decades is a magnificent tribute to its designer, J. Guthrie Brown, C.B.E., of Sir Alexander Gibb & Company, Edinburgh.

Shortly before his death last year he paid equally just tribute to the men who have manned the bridge when he presented them with a framed picture of his undoubted engineering masterpiece.

This sense of pride came over clearly when Bridgemaster George Reid told me "Imagine Hampden Park football pitch turning round on a central pivot and you'll get some idea of just how long the swing span really is. My crew feel that this bridge is very much alive," he added, as we looked downstream towards Grangemouth Docks from the control room, high above the traffic heading north and south.

Ten men man Kincardine around the clock, and standing at the controls, complete with wheel, feels exactly like being on the bridge of an ocean liner.

"When Kincardine first came into use in 1936, explained the bridgemaster, "it took 25 minutes to open to allow a vessel to sail through. Over the years we have shortened and shortened this time, until now the whole operation takes only ten or eleven minutes."

It is fortunate that the opening procedure has been so greatly speeded

Kincardine Bridge

up for Kincardine is on one of Scotland's busiest routes, with more than 10,000 vehicles a day crossing it and long delays would soon cause considerable traffic build ups as tankers sail through regularly to the oil depot at South Alloa, while the bridge was also opened several times a week to allow small naval vessels to proceed up-river to the Admiralty Ammunition Depot at Thirsk, near Stirling, until its recent closure.

Despite these frequent openings many motorists insist that they have never seen Kincardine swing into action. "When they say that to me, I tell them not to boast," says the bridgemaster, "for as sure as fate the next time they travel this way , they will find they have to wait while a ship sails through. River traffic always takes precedence."

The fact that so many drivers have never been delayed at Kincardine is exactly how the bridge crew like to keep it, but for motorists, who specially want to see it in operation, there is one special opening every week. To see it, however, they must get up very early on a Sunday morning, because at about 6 a.m. the central span is swung 360 degrees for inspection, greasing and other essential maintenance.

This procedure probably helps to account for the fact that not one item of moving machinery has ever had to be replaced in the bridge engine room, whose immaculate gleaming machinery lies hidden immediately below the main carriageway.

To motorists it is this roadway across the Forth which is the most important part of the whole bridge and the complete half-mile length linking Stirlingshire and Clackmannanshire is the responsibility of the Scottish Development Department's Roads Division, under Chief Roads Engineer Mr J. MacKenzie and his assistant Mr L. Clements, who are responsible for all of Scotland's major road bridges.

None of them, however, has quite the character of Kincardine, where, as I watched in the control room, Mr Reid rang down to his depute Mr Deans in the engine room to start the whole procedure to open the big span, which is achieved for the cost of less than 5p worth of electricty.

Each move has its own built-in safety checks to avoid the possibility of any vehicle being trapped, but the provision of closed circuit television to ensure that all traffic is clear of the descending gates, which seal off the swing span, has been rejected in favour of the previous methods of telephoned and radioed reports from the "road deck" to the control room. The staff preferred the human touch.

The Kincardine men are, however, by no means traditionalists, because from the very beginning the bridge has been to the fore in using the latest scientific aids and was one of the first places in Scotland equipped with photo electric cells which control the return to position of the bolts and wedges, which lock the central span to the north and south ends after each manoeuvre.

As the swing span drops two inches when it is opened, the photo electric cells ensure that the road surface is not only exactly in line but also absolutely level before the connecting bolts are rammed home.

Motorists often find intriguing the series of posts stuck in the mud on the Stirlingshire side. I found out from Mr Reid, that they are there for a purpose.

The southern end of the road bridge is situated right on the Central Scotland geographic fault line, and there was no bed rock on which to site the piers to support the Stirlingshire end of the bridge. Regular readings are therefore taken to note any changes in level of the south bank and the sticks in the mud form the base line for these geometry exercises.

Even the reclaiming of land well down the Forth, at Kinneil Bay on the one side and at Culross Bay on the other, has been shown by the sums carefully worked out by Mr Reid and his bridge crew to have had an effect on the tides which swirl at between six and seven knots past the bridge piers, and a concrete breakwater has been built on the south shore to provide protection.

Mentioning the accurate measurements which the staff of Kincardine Bridge have to make, I was also interested to learn from Mr Reid that every time the bridge is opened to allow a ship to sail up river to South Alloa or Thirsk, the central swing span falls by two inches and is raised again as the bolts are driven home to lock the road deck back in position, so that drivers never feel the bump.

Doing sums is only one of the many tasks, which I had never thought about, but which are a matter of daily routine to the ten-man bridge crew. Another is caring for the bridge's own gleaming fire appliance situated at the ready down on the central jetty in the middle of the river.

Fortunately, it has never had to be used, but another emergency, which the bridge staff have to deal with almost daily, is that of broken-down vehicles.

Unlike the situation on the Forth Road Bridge, motorists are not fined if they break down on Kincardine and there is not even a charge for towing them clear, the main point being to remove the hazard with the minimum delay.

The bridge's motto, emblazoned on its coat of arms is very appropriately "Look Aboot Ye," derived from the legend of Robert the Bruce and equally applicable to the bridge's modern operation, when Mr Reid interprets it as a code of conduct for his staff, demanding constant vigilance, efficiency and courtesy.

Kincardine Bridge has withstood well the tide of time since the day over 40 years ago, when its completion removed the need for the little Higgensneuk ferry, which had, until then, crossed the Forth at that point.

Chapter 3

Culross To Valleyfield

Kincardine is today overshadowed by the large electricity power station to the west and the even larger Longannet power station, with the highest chimney in the country, lying just down the river to the east.

Forgetting these two modern intrusions on the scene, it is however possible, with a little imagination, to picture Kincardine as it must have been in the seventeenth and eighteenth centuries when it was the home of as many as 50 wealthy shipowners.

In those days Kincardine was known as Newpans after the salt pans from which it derived a great deal of its trade. Much of the salt was exported to Holland, where lack of coal prevented the manufacture of salt by evaporating sea water, and this link with the Low Countries is reflected in the architecture of the houses, which have narrow gables to the street, characteristic forestairs jutting out on to the pavements and colourful red pantiles.

All these influences are seen even more attractively just along the river at nearby Culross, which the National Trust for Scotland have succeeded in preserving as a perfect example of a Scottish burgh of the seventeenth century.

Most attractive of all is the fact that the Trust have not turned the little town into a museum, but have instead helped it to find a new life by encouraging many families to come to stay in the beautifully restored white-washed houses, which are historically accurate outside, but up to the highest modern standards inside.

In the Study, home of the National Trust's representatives in Culross, two rooms have been left as they would have been when Culross was at the height of its prosperity at the start of the seventeenth century.

The turreted whitewashed Study takes its name from the fact that it was for several years used as a study by Bishop Leighton of Culross

Culross

Abbey, but it was also the home of one of the town's merchants and shipowners, and it is as such that it is today furnished.

On the old maps on the walls of the little turret room, from the windows of which the merchant must often have scanned the Forth on the lookout for his homecoming ships, it is possible to read the names of the ports with which they traded, but it is not necessary to look at any map to realise that the blue and white tiles in the living room came originally from Holland, or that the woodwork is good Baltic pine.

Many of the items in the room are however from much nearer home, and of especial interest are the brown glazed salt pig, once used to store the salt which was produced in Culross, and the flat iron baking girdle, for the making of which the hammer men of Culross were granted the Scottish monopoly in 1599 by King James VI.

James himself visited Culross on the famous occasion when he was taken by his host, the burgh's most prosperous merchant and industrialist Sir George Bruce, to inspect the Moat Pit. This coal pit was considered one of the marvels of the age because its workings ran out under the Forth and the coal was brought to the surface on a specially constructed man-made island which was surrounded by a deep-dredged moat.

One of the most profitable parts of Sir George's business was the export of coal to Holland and other parts of Europe and it was this which led him to decide to avoid the expense of land transport by mining the seams under the bed of the Forth, bringing the coal to the surface right there,out in the river, and loading it directly into waiting sailing ships.

Sir George chose as his site a point 400 yards out in Culross Bay, directly opposite Castle Hill. Work could take place only at low tide, but gradually Sir George's island began to take shape. Circular, and 60 feet in diameter, it was constructed entirely of huge blocks of stone sealed together with thick tar until they were water-tight.

In the centre a smaller circle, 18 feet wide, was left and it was in this space that Sir George ordered his miners to begin digging out what was to become the famous Moat Pit.

In 1617 King James VI visited Scotland from his court in London. He was welcomed in Fife and entertained at Culross by Sir George. The King stayed overnight at his home, The Palace, which can still be visited at Culross.

On the second day of his visit, his majesty asked to be shown the coal workings. This Sir George proudly arranged, escorting his Royal guest underground and on out through the submarine tunnel to emerge up the Moat Shaft in the middle of the bay.

As far as Sir George was concerned this should have been the highlight of the King's tour, but James was so startled at finding himself completely surrounded by water that instead of appreciating Sir George's technical prowess he immediately thought that he had become involved in some terrible plot on his life and bawled "Treason."

The King's fears were immediately allayed, however, by Sir George, who pointed out the rowing-boat moored alongside the man-made island, ready to take his majesty back to the shore.

James VI had one other strange link with the Moat Pit. At the end of March, 1625, a tremendous gale swept the Forth in the early hours one morning. Several sailors were drowned at Leith as they battled to save their ships, and at Culross the giant waves battered the thick stone sides of the Moat.

Shortly before dawn the little island's defences were eventually overwhelmed and the sea poured down the shaft of the pit. At first light Sir George, his sons, and his miners inspected the damage and found that all the colliery equipment had been swept away. The workings were extensively flooded and it was clear that the Moat Pit would never be worked again.

The great gale was taken by the local people to be an omen of ill tidings and, true enough, the final day of March brought the news from London of the King's death.

Palace of Culross

Sir George Bruce of Culross also died shortly afterwards, before he had time to devise any scheme to replace the Moat. While all traces of the Moat have long since disappeared, it is still possible to visit the Palace, as Sir George's home was known.

Whether it got its name from the fact that the King stayed there, or whether it was so called simply because it impressed the local inhabitants as the largest house in Culross, or whether yet again it is a corruption of "The Place," meaning the big house is certainly as worth a visit today as it was when King James stayed there.

From a glance, it is obvious that the Palace grew not to any plan, but simply as the fortunes of the Bruce family increased, and it is particularly interesting to note that George Bruce must indeed have been proud of his Knighthood, for he made certain that, when the new wing was added to his home, the letter "S" for "Sir" was added on top of the initials G.B. above each of the windows.

The windows themselves are also interesting because they are half shuttered. The reason for this was that when the Palace was built, glass was so thick and coarse that it was hard to see through. The bottom halves of the windows were therefore deliberately left without glass and finished instead with wooden shutters which could beopened so that the inhabitants could see out.

The windows are not the only intriguing feature of the Palace. It is also worth while paying a visit to the smallest room in the house to see what in those days was considered the most modern of conveniences, while downstairs in the cavernous stone-floored kitchen, Sir George must have been proud of the ingenious water system which he had installed.

It is, however, in the strongroom that the heart of the Palace is reached. For it was there, behind the heavy door made of iron brought back to Culross, like the iron for the famous girdles, as ballast in the sailing ships voyaging home from Gothenburg in Sweden, that the Bruce family fortune was amassed.

It was from this fortune that, when Sir George died, the stone effigy of himself, his wife and all their sons and daughters was paid for and installed in the Abbey up the hill to which Sir George had walked every Sunday morning to attend church.

On the way he no doubt kept to the crown or raised part in the middle of the causeway, as the road was called, so that he would not get his shoes wet in the gundies which flowed down either side.

On the way up to the Abbey it's worth stopping for a breather opposite Snuff Cottage, not only to admire the magnificent view right out over the Forth to Bo'ness and the Bathgate Hills rising green in the distance, but also to read the amusing inscription on the cottage walls, "Wha would a thocht it, noses would a bocht it," proclaims this eighteenth-century version of an advertising slogan for the rich brown aromatic tobacco snuff once produced there.

The climb up to Culross Abbey is a steep one, but a visit to this beautiful little church and the surrounding ruins of the monastery which once flourished there, amply repays it. Tradition has it that the Abbey was founded around 400 AD by St Serf who, after many months of travelling reached Bo'ness on the south shore of the Forth.

At that moment, the legend claims that a sunbeam lit up the hillside opposite and, taking this to be a sign from God, St Serf crossed the river, landed at where Culross now stands, and set about building his church.

Another Saint with strong links with Culross is St Mungo. For although it is as patron saint of Glasgow that Mungo is best known, it was at Culross, that he was born. His mother, Princess Thametis, daughter of Lothus, King of the Picts, finding that she was expecting a baby and fearing her father's wrath, had fled from the court in an open boat, which was eventually washed ashore at Culross.

When he grew up, Mungo carried the faith to the West of Scotland and in particular to the little village which was to grow into the city of Glasgow, a fact commemorated in the Abbey at Culross by including Glasgow's coat of arms in the stained-glass window in the apse.

The Culross church session was always on the alert against Sabbath breakers. In 1646 one George Anderson was reported to the elders accused of "running up and doune the toune in tyme of Divine Service."

Anderson confessed and promised "never to doe the lyke here after," but the session was still not satisfied, "because of his ignorance, not knowing what commandment he had broken" and so it was enacted that "if he whould not get the commandments betwixt then and that day twentie dayes, he should be brought back and scourged publicly."

The thought of the lash stinging across his bare back must have helped Anderson with his learning, for there is no record of the threatened whipping ever being administered.

Having caught him, however, the Session decided that they must take action to deter any other parishioners tempted to miss worship. They decided that they themselves must make the sacrifice of missing the minister preach and that each Sunday several of them should patrol Culross to make certain that all of the other townsfolk were safely in church.

On their first Sunday on duty the searchers, as they were called, did indeed have to go into action when they found several men gossiping in the Sandhaven in front of the Town House.

This for the time being put an end to stravaiging on the Sabbath, but there was still the problem of the children.

For the bairns of Culross were not only running about the streets, but were daring to play games down at the harbour when they should have been sitting quietly up in the church on the hill. The session met to consider this shocking behaviour and ordered that an act should be read from the pulpit on the following Lord's Day forbidding children to play either, "befor or aifter the sermon."

Even in those days there appears to have been juvenile delinquents because some time later the session had before it two laddies, including possibly one of my ancestors, young James Hendrie, for not only playing on the Sabbath but "for making Baillie Pearson's son's horse shy and throw the bairn as he rode down from the church to the waterside."

Two Culross women, Christian Blyth and Janet Cunningham who were both caught working in their gardens when they should have been at the kirk, pleaded that they had only ventured out "to pull a few sybows for their kail pots" and so they were let off with a sharp rebuke.

Even those who attended church were not safe from the censure of the session for several were punished for falling asleep during the sermon, while others were chided for making a noise while the children were saying their catechism.

This summer Sundays will be one of the busiest days of the week in Culross as thousands of tourists crowd its narrow streets to visit the Palace, the Study and the ancient Abbey and some of its residents may well wish that the old kirk session rules could be revived to ensure a peaceful Sunday.

One of the most interesting stories connected with this spot has its heart in Culross Abbey.

The story began with a duel fought far away from Fife and Scotland in the little Dutch town of Bergen-op-Zoom in the year 1613. One of the two adversaries was, however, a famous Scot of the period, Edward, Lord Bruce, and it was he who, after a fierce and bloody fight, fell mortally wounded by his enemy, the Earl of Dorset.

Lord Bruce's body was buried in the great church at Bergen-op-Zoom, but a tradition grew up in Culross, with which his family had close links, that with his dying breath his lordship had begged that his heart should be cut out and carried home to be laid to rest in the old abbey where he had so often worshipped in his youth.

It was almost 200 years later, in 1808, that Sir Robert Preston, owner of Valleyfield House, decided to put the tradition to the test by organising a thorough search of the abbey. And according to the plaque now attached to the wall in the side chapel, the heart "was found embalmed in a silver case of foreign workmanship, secured between two flat and excavated stones, clasped with iron, and was again carefully replaced and securely deposited in the spot where it was discovered."

Sir Robert Preston's search for Lord Bruce's heart was typical of his questing nature, which also led him to establish an intriguing industrial enterprise out on Preston Island, named after him, which lies close to the shore at Valleyfield.

Like most boys brought up beside a river, young Robert Preston soon learnt how to handle a boat and his favourite voyage was naturally out to the little island, which was part of his family's large Valleyfield estate.

His boyhood boating exploits made him so fond of the sea that when he grew up he made it his career, eventually becoming captain of one of the famous East India Company's ships carrying rich cargoes of spices home to London from the company's trading posts in India.

On leave in London, Sir Robert, as he was by then, was a guest at many of the parties and balls given by the city's high society and it was at one of them that he met and fell in love with the daughter of a prosperous merchant.

On his succession to the family estate in Fife, Sir Robert left the service of the East India Company and brought his young wife to stay at Low Valleyfield on the shores of the Forth. With his wide knowledge of trade and his contacts in London, he at once began to develop his estate and it was while searching for ways to do so that he remembered his childhood voyages out to little Preston Island.

While playing on it he had often stumbled over small outcrops of coal and now as he hunted for some means to improve his finances he suddenly remembered the Moat Pit in Culross Bay.

Now with a site on the island for a much better shaft than was possible out in the river and with steam pumps to cope with any inrushes of water, Sir Robert decided to repeat the experiment on Preston Island. The huge advantage which he saw for his island pit was that in those days, when the road transport of heavy loads was till practically impossible, ships could carry cargoes of coal direct from the island to London and the Continent.

Even the dross, which was not fit for export was used to feed the fires beneath the salt pans which Sir Robert also established.

Salt production on Preston Island proved so successful that a cluster of pans was soon busily at work on the shore, and the red glow from their fires burning by day and by night became a well-known beacon for sailors.

Preston Island might have continued as a profitable enterprise for many years, but it was to come to as violent an end as Sir George Bruce's Moat.

Shortly after the Preston miners, working about 250 feet down, reached the rich coals of the Lochgelly Splint, there was an explosion caused by fire damp, which killed all the men and resulted in the river breaking through into the workings.

This was not, however, the end of the Preston Island's industry. The colliery buildings were soon taken over unofficially by a much more romantic enterprise—the distilling of illicit whisky.

The island made an excellent base. It was ideally suited for smuggling the "moonshine" down river on dark nights. Output ceased suddenly, however, when the revenue men raided the island.

Today many visitors motoring along the coast road notice the ruined buildings on Preston Island and some imagine them to be the ruins of a castle, or possibly a monastery, but they are in fact the remains of the miners' houses, the colliery buildings and the salt pans set up by this early captain of Scottish industry.

Sir Robert would no doubt have been delighted to discover than Low Valleyfield in now the centre for mining operations beneath the Forth, with the Fife miners at present working right out 211 fathoms below the middle of the river bed.

I was even more intrigued to find out from the mining surveyor at

Low Valleyfield Colliery. Mr Allison, that an idea put forward in Victorian times to provide a crossing of the Forth has in fact been put into effect.

For there is now a tunnel all the way under the Forth from Low Valleyfield to Kinneil, just to the west of Bo'ness, on the opposite shore. Before car owners hasten to drive by tunnel to Fife instead of paying the toll to cross the Road Bridge, I must hasten to add Mr Allison's warning that "the tunnel is strictly for mine use only."

It is none the less kept very busy for Mr Allison explained that none of the coal dug out by the miners at his colliery is brought up the shaft at Low Valleyfield. All of it is transported by narrow gauge electric railway and incline tracks right across beneath the river and is brought to the surface at Kinneil, which possesses the most modern washing and other processing facilities.

Mr Allison went on to tell me that the distance between Low Valleyfield and Kinneil is just under three and a half miles. The reason for this is that the underground workings, which were joined up by the mining engineers to link the two collieries, do not follow a direct line.

A much bigger difficulty for the engineers was the big difference between the levels of the underground workings of the two collieries, those on the Fife side being on average 1250 feet deep while those at Kinneil go down to more than 1800 feet.

The problems were overcome, however, and the Forth Tunnel, or the "Funnel," as it was inevitably nicknamed, was completed when mine driver Martin "Tiger" Shaw broke through the last few inches of sandstone on April 30, 1964. Kinneil Colliery's manager David Archibald greeted his opposite number Norman Wallace with the remark: "I hope you've plenty of coal for me, " and the tunnel 1800 feet beneath the bed of the Forth has indeed done much to ensure the continued operation of the Bo'ness pit by providing it with a flow of coal from Fife at times when its own workings proved difficult to operate.

Thus while the Victorian suggestion of a tunnel beneath the Forth has in a way come to pass, another proposed alternative to the Road Bridge has been almost completely forgotten except by some of the older generation.

Forty years ago, an ambitious plan was put forward to dam the River Forth, and for a time it seemed as though its supporters would triumph over those fighting for the Road Bridge which now spans the river.

Kinneil Pit, Bo'ness

The Forth Dam Scheme was the brain-child of two West Lothian men, architect Mr Matthew Steele and Bo'ness hotel owner Mr John Jeffrey. The advantages which they claimed for their dam were many and varied, but during the work-starved years of the early 1930's one of the most persuasive was their contention that building a dam would provide far more jobs than the erection of a road bridge, for the thousands of local men who were "on the dole".

They pointed out that a bridge would be built of steel, which would be manufactured outside the area, and that the steel would have to be erected by skilled men, brought specially to Queensferry, probably from England. On the other hand, Mr Jeffrey and Mr Steele claimed that building a huge barrage dam would provide thousands of jobs for unskilled labourers and would also create work for the many West Lothian miners who were unemployed, as thousands of tons of whinstone would be required to form the barrage.

They also pointed out that many more men could have been given work demolishing the district's numerous ugly old coal and shale bings to provide more material for the dam, which was to span the Forth near the site of the new Road Bridge between North and South Queensferry.

Behind the dam the water level was to be controlled so that it would always be several feet above the natural high tide mark, and the Forth from Queensferry to Stirling would be transformed into an enormous artificial lake. All the hideous black mad-flats which mar the beauty of the river at low tide would be completely hidden and Mr Jeffrey had visions of his man-made lake becoming a highly popular water playground for the whole of Central Scotland. He suggested that, as on the Swiss lakes, and on the Clyde, small steamers or motor launches could provide regular services to the picturesque little villages, such as Culross and Dunmore on either side of the Forth. Their mud-silted harbours would be given a new lease of life if the water level were raised by the dam.

Together with fast water bus services, the new road along the dam would do much to open up West Fife.

Even more important, however, than the dam's effect on tourism and transport would be its effect on the industrial development of the whole of the Forth Valley. Constant high water would enable ships to enter or leave Grangemouth and Bo'ness Docks at any time without any costly delays waiting for the tide.

Deeper water, it was also stressed, would help Grangemouth's shipbuilding industry, as it would enable it to launch larger vessels.

During the 1930's when the dam project was under discussion sea-planes were much in the news, and as part of their campaign Mr Jeffrey and Mr Steele pointed out that the huge artificial lake behind their barrage would make an ideal landing area for these planes. They also stressed that their proposed dam would in no way damage Rosyth as a naval dockyard, as even the largest warship would be able to pass through the lock which they planned to build in the centre of the barrage to raise vessels from the normal river level to that of the lake.

Another advantage which Jeffrey and Steele claimed for their project was that the water dammed up behind the barrage could be used to create hydro-electric power for all the Forth Valley towns. The millions of gallons of water would also be available for industrial use which would be a big inducement in bringing new factories to West Lothian, Stirlingshire, and part of Fife. This use of the water would not spoil the amenity value of the Forth "lake" as purification plants would be built.

The coming of war in 1939 put an end to any schemes to span the Forth either by dam or by bridge and when the campaign for a road bridge began again after 1945, the alternative suggested was no longer the barrage but an under-water tunnel.

Recently, however, the whole question of the feasibility of constructing giant dams has been raised again by the putting forward of proposals that they might be the ideal means of bridging the Solway, Morecambe Bay, and even the English Channel. Perhaps it may yet be proved that the two West Lothian businessmen, were much more far-seeing than their critics during the 1930's believed.

Chapter 4

Witches Of The Forth

Among the villages which would have benefited most if the dam—which was planned for almost the same site as the present Road Bridge—had been constructed and the water level raised, would have been Torryburn, whose mud-silted bay would have been completely transformed. Torryburn would certainly have had an off-beat attraction to offer its holidaymakers—it's long history of witchcraft.

It was during the 1690's that the "Witch Fever," as it was known, gripped the whole of Torryburn as the village minister, the Rev. Allan Logan, a dedicated self-appointed witchfinder-general, devoted himself wholeheartedly to the task of stamping out "all trafficking with the Devil and His invisible world".

Time after time Mr Allan called his kirk session to hear cases of alleged black magic, until one of the old women of the parish, Helen Kay, was brave or foolish ėnough to voice the opinion of many of the other members of his congregation that the minister "was daft on the witches".

Furious, Mr Allan ordered her to be brought before the session and had her sentenced to be publicly rebuked in front of the whole village.

Undeterred by old Helen's criticism, Mr Allan continued with his witch trials, the most notorious of which ended in the death of Lilias Adie. Lilias was arrested by the Baron Baillie of Torryburn in 1704 and was accused of being "in compact with the Devil".

At her trial Lilias confessed that she had met the "Prince of Darkness" on several occasions on the road just outside Torryburn. It is easy to imagine the hush in the court as Lilias was urged by the Rev. Mr Allan to go on and describe "the De'il himself". With every eye upon her, Lilias declared that "He was wearing a hat on his head, and his feet were cloven, like the feet of a stirk".

With this damning evidence given against herself, there could be no other verdict than one of guilty. Normally the Torrburn witches were transported to the Witch Knowe at Dunfermline, where they were publicly burned at the stake — no fewer than six women being executed in one three-month period. But Lilias was saved from such a fate as she died in the jail at Torryburn and, as an ex-communicated person, was buried on the seashore within the high-water mark.

There the tragic story of Lilias might have ended, but 100 years ago her remains were dug up and her skull was purchased by Mr Joseph Paton, of Dunfermline.

Mr Paton allowed Dr W. B. Dow to examine it, and the doctor wrote the final chapter in the story when, in September, 1884, he delivered a lecture on the case to the Fife Medical Association. He declared that the skull was so abnormally small that he had no hesitation in declaring that Lilias had suffered from a diseased brain.

To the townsfolk of Bo'ness, witches and warlocks were very real indeed and very much in the news at Hallowe'en 1679, for no fewer than six had been arrested within the last few days in the old burgh.

Rumours of dreadful bloodcurdling happenings practised at dead of night swept through the town, as the warlock, Willaim Draw, and five witches, Bessie Vicar, Margaret Hamilton, Margaret Pringle, Annabel Thomsone, and a second Margaret Hamilton, were accused of

witchcraft after they had given both their bodies and souls to the Devil.

Stories quickly spread of how all six had met the De'il at the Murestan to the south of Bo'ness on the unlucky night of October 13 and of how they had danced in the darkness, while the Devil played the pipes.

Worse still — it was said that they had plotted with the Devil to destroy Andrew Mitchell, the son of John Mitchell of Kinneil, a small hamlet to the west of Bo'ness.

As the local people crowded out into the narrow winding streets, Craw and the five women, all of whom were widow's, were taken to the thick stone walled tolbooth in South Street, where they were imprisoned to await their trial.

The charges against them were considered so serious that the Scottish Privy Council ordered eight of the most prominent gentlemen of the county, including Cornwall of Bonhard Castle, Robert Hamilton of Dechmont, and three well-known Advocates, to act as Commissioners and try the case.

At last, on December 19, all was ready for the trial and the six accused were brought into the Court to hear the evidence of their townsfolk against them.

The trial began on that cold winter morning with the reading of the indictment.

It began: "Yee and ilk ane or you ar indytted and accused that wheras the cryme of witchcraft is declaired to be ane horrid abominable and capital cryme, punishable with the paines of death and confiscation of moveables, nevertheless it is of veritee that you have committed and are gwyltie of the said cryme of witchcraft in so far as ye have entered into paction with the Devill, the enemie of your salvation and have renounced our blessed Lord and saviour and your baptisme and have given yourselves, both soulles and bodies to the Devill".

After they had been accused of having had several meetings with the Devil, the individual crimes of Craw and of each of the five women were solemnly read out. One, Annable Thomsone, was declared to have first met the Devil while walking from Linlithgow to Bo'ness, when he approached her in the "lykness of ane black man".

The Devil had apparently come right into Borrowstounness, (as Bo'ness was called), for it was claimed that Margaret Hamilton had met him at the town well and later, on several occasions, in her own home.

There the Devil had drunk ale and had given her a five merk gold piece which afterwards turned into a small stone.

More evidence was brought that after Margaret Pringle had promised to follow the Devil, he had taken hold of her right hand which for eight days afterwards had been "grievouslie pained," until the Devil returned and shook it again, whereupon it was immediately cured.

As the day wore on, the courtroom with its low ceiling and its small windows became darker and darker and when the tapers and candles were lit they sent ghostly shadows flickering up the walls.

At last, by late afternoon all the evidence had been heard and the members of the jury retired. When they returned to the courtroom it was to announce that they had found all guilty of witchcraft.

Immediately the verdict was given, amid the shrieks and wails of the prisoners, the Commissioners pronounced sentence upon the miserable six, ordering that they were to be publicly burned to death for their evil deeds.

Carefully the Clerk of the Court wrote down the instructions of the Commissioners about how the sentence was to be carried out.

All six were to be taken to the "ordinary place of execution" and there "on the 23rd of December between the hours of two and four in the afternoon" they were to be "wirried at a steack till they be dead and thereafter to have their bodies burnt to ashes".

The Baylie Principal of the Regalitie of Borrowstounness and his Deputes were at once instructed to make all the necessary arrangements for the mass execution and to make certain that it was carried out in all its dreadful detail.

Thus, four days later the five witches and John Craw the warlock were led out of their cells in the old tolbooth for the last time and were taken along the Corbiehall, as one of the streets in Bo'ness is still called, to the flat stretch of ground on the shore of the River Forth to the west of the town.

There, the stakes had been set up in readiness and the fires were soon lit. By the time the pale winter sun had dipped below the hills on that December afternoon, the executions were all over, the fires had burnt themselves down to the glowing embers, justice had been done . . . and Bo'ness was rid of its poor innocent "witches".

Another Bo'ness woman, Anna Wood, who was also accused of witchcraft, could hardly be blamed for escaping before her trial was concluded. Indeed, the townsfolk were not surprised that she escaped, for the evidence against her stated that she had the power to turn herself into a black cat or take flight as a black bird.

Black cats are considered good luck symbols, but in Scotland this was definitely not always the case.

For, in bygone times, black cats were always associated with witches and warlocks. They were feared and so, too, were their cats, to such an extent that in many areas farmers would abandon trips to market if one crossed their path, as they were convinced that they would no longer get good prices for their goods.

Another animal which Scots of previous centuries were certain had been possessed by witches was the hare, for, why else would they behave in such a mad fashion?

Nor was it only animals about which the country folk of Scotland had their superstitions. Birds, too, were sometimes viewed with suspicion. Flocks of gulls seen far inland from the sea were always considered a clear sign of a storm brewing. Corbies or crows were often associated with death, probably because of their jet black plummage and great flapping wings, or possibly because they were often seen hovering over dead lambs or other dead animals in the fields and hedgerows.

Many Scots believed that when witches took to the air they often took on the form of crows so that they would not be spotted flying on their evil missions. Evidence of this was given in 1704 when Anna a young serving wench was accused of witchcraft and tried by the Carriden Kirk session.

Her main accuser was a sailor called Robert Nimmo. Nimmo, declared that one pitch-black night he was walking home alone to Bo'ness from Linlithgow when he was suddenly surrounded by Anna and five other witches. No matter how fast he ran through the darkness they danced menacingly around him.

When he reached the summit of the Erngath Hills, midway between the two towns, he prayed that he could out-distance them as he raced down the slope towards his home on the shores of the Forth at Carriden, but they prevented him from doing so by using their evil powers. For as he neared "Sir William Seton's farm, Park Dyke, at Northbank," where they might have been spotted, they changed into muckle black craws and flapped threateningly all around him.

Nimmo then went on to claim that the crows flew with him all the way down to the salt pans at Grangepans; where he actually saw Anna change back into her role of servant girl.

With this kind of evidence against her, Anna looked in dire danger of being sentenced to be burned at the stake on the shores of the Forth, as happened to six other local witches and one warlock, so it is hardly surprising that she seized an opportunity to escape and was never seen again in the town.

Another of the Forth's most famous cases of Black magic took place at Hallowe'en 1590 when, as darkness fell over the little East Lothian town of Prestonpans and the night sky was lit only by the ruddy glow of the fires of the old burgh's famous salt pans, a procession of more than 200 local women made its way down to the harbourside.

At its head was respected local schoolmaster James Cunningham. But the lessons he was to teach them were however, very different from those which he whipped into their bairns by day . . . for once darkness fell he exchanged his role of God-fearing dominie for that of the Satan worshipping Dr Fian.

Once on the quayside Dr Fian supervised the embarkation of the women into the small boats, because on that "Allhallon-Even" they were to voyage down the Firth to North Berwick to meet no less a personage than the De'il.

Excitement ran high as the fishing boats nosed their way out of the harbour and the shrieks and laughter of the women could be heard as they emptied the flagons of wine and ale which they had taken with them as they headed for "the Kirke of North Barrick," where the Devil was alleged to await their coming.

After landing at North Berwick, despite the exhortations of Dr Fian that they must hurry, the women of his coven began to dance and sing on the quayside. The voyage from Prestonpans had already taken much longer than he had anticipated and in the end he led them still dancing to the church, where their noise and clamour was quickly chilled.

For there by the pulpit was the black-clad figure of the Devil. Today historians believe that this terrifying apparition "with goat-like beard and flowing tail" was Frances Stewart, Earl of Bothwell, for he had a throne to gain if the Scottish king died childless and an attempt to kill James VI was, in fact, to be the work of that dark night.

First, however, the figure by the pulpit ranted and raved at Dr Fian and his followers for their late arrival. Then by the flickering light of the candles some of the women later declared, in a horrible shrivelled severed human hand, he produced from below his cloak a waxen doll, which was to represent King James in the rites which followed.

Wrapping the image in a piece of linen, obtained by one of the young serving wenches at the Palace of Holyrood and declared to have been worn recently by the king, the black-robed figure began piercing it with needles, while each of the women in turn wished death upon the king.

It was, however, the death of James Cunningham, alias Dr Fian, which resulted from that coven's meeting because King James soon heard of the events and having forced the truth out of one of his servants Agnes Sampson, a witch trial was quickly summoned in the Tolbooth in the Royal Mile.

The Earl of Bothwell did not wait for the trial to begin, but fled to Italy. For Dr Fian there was, however, no escape.

With a torture chamber set up in an anteroom to help remind witnesses of the black magic that had been practised, there was no lack of evidence set before the king and the commissioners.

There could be only one verdict — guilty — and days later Dr Fian was led from the Tolbooth to be strangled by the executioner after which his body was burned.

When even the king believed so implicitly in the powers of evil it was hardly surprising that witch trials flourished in many Scottish towns. In Stirling in 1617 one Jonet Andersone confessed, "that ane tailyour in Falkirk called Sandie wear, cam to her with ane sark on ane bairne of the Chamberlane of Kinneil and did seik the death of the bairn".

Kinneil, which lies just to the west of Bo'ness, has another link with the supernatural. For Kinneil House, the home of the Hamilton family, who are said to have been granted all the lands in the area as a reward for the way in which they fought against the English prior to and during the Battle of Bannockburn, is said to be haunted.

At first the house consisted simply of a square keep, whose massive thick stone walls can still be seen, but later in the seventeenth century when more peaceful times had come to Scotland it was greatly expanded by Anna, Duchess of Hamilton, into the impressive building which West Lothian's earliest historian, Sir Robert Sibbald, described as "This Palace of Kinneil".

It was to this mansion, set on a hill high above the Forth, that the lovely Lady Lilbourne came in the year 1651. She was the wife of

General Lilbourne, one of Oliver Cromwell's commanders, who with Kinneil requisitioned as his headquarters was entrusted with the task of ensuring that Scotland remained loyal to the new republic which Cromwell had established following the execution of King Charles I.

But it was within his own headquarters that General Lilbourne was to find rebellion.

When he was ordered north to Scotland, the General had just married Alice. Obviously reluctant to be parted from her for what could be a lengthy period, he decided to bring his young bride to Kinneil with him. Unfortunately the marriage did not prove a happy one. Bitterly homesick, Lady Alice repeatedly asked to be allowed to return to England but the General refused and instead, in harshest military style, ordered that she should be locked in a tiny attic room until she gave in and obeyed him.

Lady Lilbourne was not, however, to be so easily quelled and late one night succeeded in escaping from her way out of the house and then, according to local tradition, clad only in a diaphanous flowing white nightgown, she fled down the long dark tree-lined drive towards the lights of Bo'ness. But before she could reach them her husband and the Kinneil servants, who had given chase, caught up with her and she was soon dragged back to the big house.

Even after this experience Lady Lilbourne would not submit to her husband, so once again she was imprisioned in the little room set high on the west side of the house, overlooking the deep rocky ravine which with the fast flowing Gil Burn had provided the original Kinneil Keep with its main defensive feature. By this time, however, Lady Alice, was desperate and flung herself out of the narrow window, plunging almost 200 feet to her death on the rocks below.

Lady Lilbourne's tragic death did not end her connection with Kinneil, for ever since the White Lady, as she has been called because of her billowing white nightdress, is said to have haunted the old house, her shrieks and screams echoing on dark nights through its now ruined halls and passageways.

A small bridge leads across the deep Gil Burn ravine where Lady Lilbourne fell to her death and on to one of the estate's other interesting ruins, that of the historic Kinneil Parish Kirk, with its many interesting gravestones carved with symbols indicating what the people buried there once worked at.

Another stone which always attracts the attention of visitors is the large Celtic cross unearthed a few years ago at Kinneil which proved that, this site has been a place of worship since earliest Christian times. Kinneil Kirk continued in use until Covenanting days, when the minister and his congregation were forced out to hold secret conventicles on the wooded hillside above the big house.

In Kinneil House itself, other religious relics are the large murals, believed to have been painted by travelling Italian artists. These depict several Biblical stories, including those of the Good Samaritan and the Prodigal Son.

Chapter 5

Land From The Sea

Compared with the River Clyde, the Forth has often been described as the ugly sister because of the black mud flats which marr its veins, and nowhere is this seen clearer than at Kinneil.

Now, however, these areas may prove their worth in gold, for the largest of them in Kinneil Bay is being considered as the ideal flat site for a vast new oil-related complex which will rival the giant refinery at adjacent Grangemouth.

The idea of reclaiming Kinneil Bay from the river is, however, by no means a new one. It goes back all of 500 years to the days of James Cadzow, first Lord Hamilton, of Kinneil.

Looking down from the battlements of his fortified peel tower, Hamilton must often have thought how much value the acres of Kinneil Bay could add to his already rich estates — if only he could wrest them from the shallow waters of the Forth, because in the end be launched what must have been one of Scotland's first reclamation schemes. The duke even managed to obtain a special royal blessing for his ambitious scheme from King James III as he was married to the king's sister, Mary Stewart.

Despite his enthusiasm. Hamilton found that reclamation took longer than he had anticipated, because he depended on a special system of stone dykes incorporating ingeniously designed drainage holes.

His idea was that at high tide the river would flood over the top of his walls. Then as the tide ebbed the water escaped again, through the drains, while the mud and debris brought in on the incoming tide were deposited behind the barrier. Thus with every high tide the land behind the dykes rose by a fraction of an inch, until at last in 1474 Lord Hamilton's patience was rewarded— he was able to farm his new acres for the first time.

To show his gratitude to God for this great bounty. Hamilton announced that all rents from this unusual addition to his estates would go to support the little church and hospital, which had been recently built on another part of his family's extensive lands at the village of Shotts in Lanarkshire.

Two hundred years later it was not the local landowners with estates around Kinneil Bay, but Dutch engineers, who suggested another attempt to seize more acres from the Forth, Encouraged by their successes in Holland, they visited many of the estate owners between Queensferry and Kincardine, explaining how they could add to their estates not only good farming land, but land suitable for the building of new towns and harbours.

The Scottish landowners were, however, less than enthusiastic. They believed in those days when overland transport was difficult in summer and well-nigh impossible in winter because of the state of the roads that it was their water frontage which endowed their estates with much of their value. Offers by the Dutch engineers to extend fields out into the Forth were viewed with suspicion as the landowners feared that the Dutchmen, instead of adding to the richness of the estates would detract from it by meddling with the course of the river.

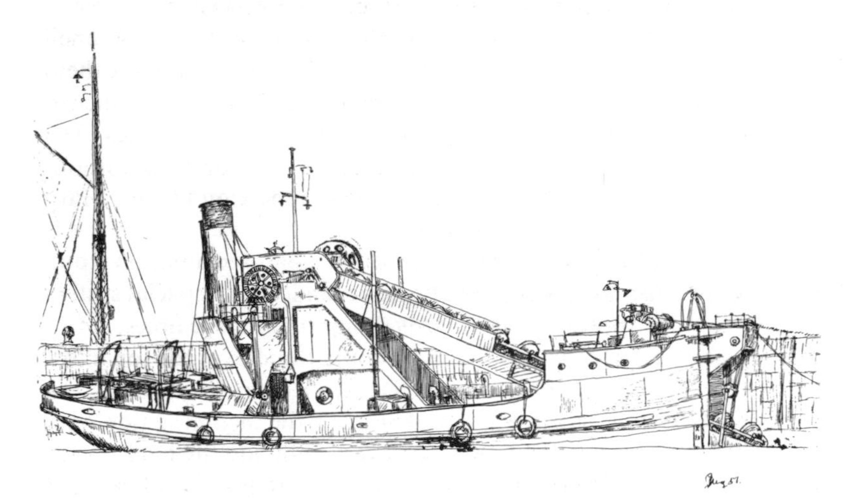

A familiar sight on the river in years gone by were the Bucket Dredgers for which the Forth's famous mud flats provided never ending work.

Permission was refused and the engineers returned home.

In 1710 the idea was revived by West Lothian's earliest historian, Sir Robert Sibbald of Kipps Castle, near Linlithgow, when he wrote: "It is thought that by reclaiming the area of Kinneil Bay, that this might make the narrow part of the Firth deeper and the navigation to the upper part of the river more commodious".

Later in the eighteenth century, the Dutch reclamation experts returned, but it was to a site farther up river, between Grangemouth and Kincardine that they devoted their attention with considerable success. Today this area is known as Skinflats and many local people consider that they are unfortunate to have been blessed with one of Scotland's ugliest place names.

What they fail to realise is that the name is not Scottish at all, but Dutch, and that by adopting it the engineers from Holland were expressing their delight at their success in winning these acres from the sea. For in Dutch the name means "The Beautiful Plains," and looking out from the little Dutch Inn at Bothkennar, which is a lasting reminder of the area's links with the Low Countries, this sweep of flat green farming country does indeed look attractive, especially if seen on a summer evening as the sun sets over the river beyond Kincardine Bridge.

While land reclamation has beautified the river by covering up its oozing black mud flats, or slob lands as they are known, it was the growth of local industries with their resultant waste products which provided land reclamation with its greatest boost.

At Bo'ness, waste from the coal pits, cinders from the fire which burned continuously by day and by night beneath the salt pans, and slag from the local iron works, were dumped into the river.

Many of these works were owned by Henry Cadell, of Grange, one of Scotland's earliest geologists. He took a keen interest in all this dumping and the effect which it was having and in the end decided to use all this waste to reclaim the whole length of shore between Kinneil to the west of Bo'ness and Carriden to the east. Within years a broad ribbon of flat land fronted the town of Bo'ness which formerly had been crowded into the little area around the harbour.

At first the new land was not firm enough for building, but it provided an ideal site for the new imported pit prop industry, which brought tremendous prosperity to nineteenth-century Bo'ness and earned the town the nickname "Proptown" as a forest of sawn tree trunks grew up all over the reclaimed lands.

While Cadell of Grange used his acres from the sea to encourage new industries, much further up river beyond Stirling, an ambitious effort was made to reclaim land for agricultural use.

It was in the year 1766 that the famous Scottish law lord, Lord Kames, became owner of Blairdrummond; but although his new estate was large it was not very prosperous because almost 2000 acres of it was covered with a thick layer of springy peat moss up to twelve feet deep in places, which made any kind of farming completely impossible.

Lord Kames had, however, had some experience of land reclamation on his other estates and he therefore determined to rid Blairdrummond of its blanket of moss below which he was certain lay good, rich alluvial soil which would be excellent for agricultural use. The problem was of course how to remove the vast 121 mile-long layer of mossy peat to reach the soil beneath. Several earlier attempts to remove the moss by digging it up had all been defeated by the enormity of the task.

Lord Kames therefore set about looking for some other quicker method and finally decided that the only feasible way was to use water power in order to wash away all the peat out into the nearby river Forth. Soon labourers were hired to dig canals down which to float the moss to the river, but although Lord Kames was able to show that his idea worked it appeared that he would have to give it up, because of the tremendous expense.

It was then, just as it seemed that Blairdrummond Moss must remain as unproductive as ever, that Lord Kames thought up a way to get all the work done free.

He knew that in the Highlands the terrible Clearances had begun and hundreds of the crofters were being forced to leave their homes to make way for the sheep which were more profitable and required less labour. Lord Kames reasoned that, rather than emigrate to America and Canada as many of them were doing or coming south to work in Glasgow, many of them would much prefer to find new land to farm, and as they were well used to labouring outdoors in all weathers he reckoned that they would be the ideal people to rid his estate of its mossy blanket.

He, therefore, decided to offer them 10-acre crofts with fixity of tenure and freedom from rent for the first seven years it they would in return promise to clear their holdings of moss. To make his offer even more attractive to the shrewd Highland crofters he, in his turn, went on to promise them that until they could grow food to feed themselves he would provide them with eight bushels of meal a year and, of course, as he pointed out, there would always he plenty of peat to light their fires.

It was in 1769 that the first of the Highlanders arrived at Blairdrummond, much to the terror of the local inhabitants who were as frightened of the Moss lairds as they sarcastically called the newcomers from the north as they would have been of the lions of two centuries later. Terrible rumours spread before the coming of the Moss Lairds that those Highland crofters were little better than savages of immense strength who were frequently violent, especially when drunk, which was their usual state.

To begin with the Moss Lairds did not help improve relations for they spoke no English and formed their own little Highland Gaelic-speaking community, living in dwellings unlike anything that the people of the area had ever seen before. These were even more simple and more primitive than anything which the crofters had been used to in the Highlands, but with very good reason. For they very soon discovered that as much as a footstep on the moss was enough to make it vibrate for up to fifty yards and a stone or brick built cottage would have collapsed as if hit by an earthquake. It was true Scottish guile, therefore, and not laziness which caused the Moss Lairds to cut their first homes right out of the peat moss itself.

How they managed this is described in detail in an old book about the area called "The Story of the Forth," by the late Henry M. Cadell, of Grange who was a well-known early Scottish geologist. To begin with the Moss Laird and his wife and family set to work to cut a deep wide trench right down through the moss all the way round the site which they had chosen for their new home. Within the square trench this left a large solid block of peat and it was from this that they scooped out their house, just as "a child hollows out the heart of a turnip to make a lantern," as Cadell so graphically describes it.

At first the walls of the peat houses were as high as twelve feet, but as the peat dried out they shrunk until they were only about five feet high and between three and four feet thick. They were roofed with wood supplied free by Lord Kames, and once they were thatched with the heather which grew all around it was hard to tell them apart from the surrounding countryside. It was scarcely surprising, therefore, that the people around Doune and Thornhill thought the Moss Lairds' homes only fit for wild animals, but the Moss Lairds did not worry for inside the one small dark low-ceilinged room which they had thus formed for themselves it was snug and warm and, being so low, very well protected from the fiercest wind which blew across the plain of the moss lands.

Gradually, however, as they won their battle with the moss at Blairdrummond they replaced their original homes with the more usual stone cottage. By this time, too, their hard work and law-abiding conduct proved to their Lowland neighbours that they need not really lock up all their valuables and their daughters as they had at first worriedly predicted. Thus the barriers between the Highlanders and the local people were broken down and slowly the social stigma of being a Moss Laird disappeared; today it is considered rather an honour to claim descent from them.

Lord Kames, who was over seventy when he began his ambitious experiment at Blairdrummond, died in 1782, but his son, George Home Drummond, continued to encourage the Moss Lairds. He built new roads to open up the district and provide a link with Stirling and provided prizes of ploughs and bags of seeds for those who cleared the largest area in the shortest time, but most important of all he made the Moss Lairds task easier by constructing a huge water wheel close to the point where the Teith joins the Forth thus making available to them far greater water power to wash away the moss.

Several other landowners around Blairdrummond copied his example and by 1811 as many as 150 Moss Lairds and their families, making a total of around 900 people, were all engaged in clearing more and more of Blairdrummond Moss, Cardross Moss, Flanders Moss and Kincardine-in-Menteith Moss.

The Moss Lairds added to their income by cutting the peat and selling it in Stirling and other towns in the area and encouraged by George Drummond, who agreed to pay part of the dominie's £15 salary, they managed to afford a school for their children to attend.

So, over the years, the Moss Lairds became integrated into the community and by working hard were able to buy livestock and lay the foundations for the prosperous farms, which are still seen by visitors to Blairdrummond's wildlife park.

Another eighteenth century landowner who expanded his estate by reclaiming land from the Forth was Lord Keith of Tulliallan.

To begin with, there was too much salt in the soil to grow anything, but after three years he was able to grow grass and seven years later the new riverside fields began bearing good crops of barley, beans, oats, potatoes and wheat.

In his first experiment Lord Kames succeeded in reclaiming 150 acres for a cost of only £7,000. He was so encouraged that he decided to go on to reclaim another 200 acres down the Fife side of the Forth, where Longannet Power Station now stands. Appropriately, it is ash from the electric power station which is now being pumped farther down stream to reclaim even more land at Culross Bay.

Chapter 6

Oil Boom

Back on the opposite shore, where the Forth reclamations story began all these years ago, at Kinneil Bay, the river may soon be forced to yield even more of its acres to form what will become one of Scotland's most important industrial sites. For Grangemouth's giant oil refinery has now grown to such an extent that it recently expanded across the River Avon, which marks both the eastern boundary between Central and Lothian Region and between Grangemouth and Bo'ness.

The erection of these huge oil tanks on the flat land edging Kinneil Bay, just within the burgh of Bo'ness, means that history has come full circle, because long before the modern tankers sailed up the Forth to the docks at Grangemouth, sailing ships were regularly bringing cargoes of oil to the old harbour at Bo'ness.

Unlike the crude oil of today the oil of the eighteenth and nineteenth centuries arrived in form of blubber stored in the holds of the "whalers". These small sailing vessels, with their specially strengthened wooden hulls, each spring set sail from Bo'ness, or Borrowstounness as it was then correctly known, to voyage to the Arctic to hunt the whale. If they were lucky, they returned home each autumn with their rich cargoes.

Scotland's interest in the whale oil industry began in the year 1750 when the Government offered a special bounty of £2 per ton to encourage this highly dangerous and risky hunt in the icy waters of the Arctic.

This meant that the first 333-ton Scottish whaler to set sail was guaranteed an income of £666 even if her harpooner failed to catch a single "fish" as the great ocean monsters were always, but erroneously, termed.

The first voyage must, however, have been successful, for six whalers set sail the following year, and by 1756 the fleet had increased to sixteen.

Sailing ships crowded the dock when the Port of Bo'ness was at its peak.

As the industrial revolution progressed over the next half century the demand for oil soared, and during the years after the end of the Napoleonic Wars in 1815, Leith, Bo'ness, Burntisland, Kirkcaldy, Dundee, Montrose, Aberdeen, Peterhead, Banff, Kirkwall and Greenock all had their squat broad-beamed square rigged whalers. A detailed model of one such vessel with her specially reinforced bow to withstand the pressure of the Arctic ice, can be seen in the Royal Scottish Museum in Edinburgh.

By tradition all the whalers from each port set sail together on the same day for company on the long voyage north, and it was always a very emotional occasion. In Bo'ness for instance crowds from Linlithgow and other surrounding towns joined the local folk who thronged the quayside to watch the crews of the whalers in their new rigouts of thick knitted navy jerseys, black waterproofs, high leather sea boots and fisherman-like bonnets, boarded their vessels.

Excitement reached its peak as they were joined by the harpooners for it was upon this elite band that the whole success of the expedition depended, but it was an excitement mixed with tears for wives and girl friends in the crowds knew full well that they might never see their loved ones again for no one ever underestimated the dangers involved in the hunting of the whale and even if they did survive they would not see them again for almost six months.

When all the whalers were ready to put to sea they all fired off the little cannon which they carried in the sterns. This was the signal for the crowd to break and run up the steep braes behind Bo'ness to watch as the "Jean," "The Home Castel," "The Ratler," and the lucky "Success" sailed away down the Forth and out of sight, into the North Sea.

The Bo'ness fleet stayed together, as did those of the other East Coast ports until they reached the hunting grounds of the Faroes and Iceland. Once there it was every vessel for herself and a constant watch was kept from the crow's nest in the hope of being first to shout "Whale Ho".

Immediately the signal was given the whaler launched her six or eight small boats each crewed by four oarsmen, the all-important harpooner poised in the bow and the coilsman at the ready in the stern. As the name suggests it was the coilsman's duty to make sure that the line attached to the eight-foot long wooden and barbed metal tipped harpoon ran free, when the harpooner launched his vicious weapon.

These primitive harpoons lacked any kind of explosive charge in their tips and so it was necessary to be at very close range before they had any effect on the huge sixty to eighty foot whales which were often caught. Usually several strikes were necessary and there was always the danger that the enraged whale would capsize the small boat as it thrashed in agony or tried to escape by swimming under the nearest ice floe.

One blow from a whale's tail was enough to smash a small boat like a match box and once in the freezing water there was little hope for any of the men. It was always said that whalers always deliberately refused to learn to swim. It was quicker that way.

When a harpooner was successful in making a kill all the other small boats from a mother ship raced to his aid to help tow the catch alongside. Even when the whale was safely back at the mother ship there was no time to be lost for the carcass would only float for a limited time. No matter how exhausted the crew were, they had immediately to begin the flensing.

For this they swapped their sea boots for others with metal spikes in the soles , and wearing those they clambered over the side and down on to the slippery back of the whale. There, using specially shaped knives, they cut through the flesh and ripped it back to reveal the all-important six to twelve inch layer of oily blubber.

This was cut into brick-like oblongs which were tossed on to the deck to be stowed in the ship's holds. Unlike Dutch and Danish whalers the Scots never processed the blubber in the Arctic but always brought it back to be boiled in Scotland's earliest oil refineries, which existed in all of their home towns.

Each whale which was caught was carefully noted in the ship's log and indicated with a drawing of a whale's tail in the margin, as can be seen in the logs carefully preserved in the Museum of Fisheries at Anstruther in Fife.

It was, however, not only battles with the whales which were recorded in many ships' logs, but fights amongst the crew. For the long months cooped up in one communal cabin inevitably took their toll of frayed tempers.

The other battles which the whalers were often called upon to fight were against the ice, because it only needed a bad season, a poor catch and a decision to linger one day too many to leave a whaler trapped for the whole winter.

For those of the whalers which did enjoy a good season and did return safely the prizes were high. The largest cargo of blubber ever landed in Scotland was brought ashore by the Resolution of Peterhead, which caught forty-four whales in 1814. When this was processed it yielded oil to the value of £10,000, which was a princely sum in the nineteenth century, and to this was added a further £1,000 raised from a roup of bones, for the long flexible whale-bones were in great demand for a variety of uses as varied as making furniture, producing waist-pinching stays for fashionable ladies, and even more painful pandybats, long leather covered cane like implements with which Irish school masters chastised their erring scholars.

The whalers, and especially the harpooners, were continually in demand to spin their yarns about their adventures in the Arctic. But the winter months were not holidays, because, besides overhauling and preparing their ships for the next season, most of them worked in the two local whale oil factories.

The main whale oil works belonged to John Anderson, a prosperous Bo'ness merchant banker, who also owned many of the whalers and who was often called the "Uncrowned King of Bo'ness". It stood on the side of Tidings Hil and was reached from the old town clustered round the harbour, by a steep road called the Wynd.

The large catches and high profits of the 1860s had ironically sounded the death knell of the Scottish whaling industry as without any form of protection the Arctic whales were beginning to die out.

For a time the Arctic whalers did fight back by greatly increasing their efficiency through the introduction of steam whalers. To begin with the old sailors declared that steam whalers could never succeed as the noise of their propellors would either frighten the whales away or soon act as a warning signal to them.

Their fears proved unfounded and soon the "Narwhal" and the other steam whalers were hunting in waters considered too dangerous by the masters of the old sailing vessels. like the Davis Straits and Melville Bay.

Steam also increased the range of the whalers all the way to the fiords of Greenland, but even more important was the fact that their increased speed and greater sea-worthiness made it possible for them to sail earlier in the year and thus fit in two round trips each season.

Despite all efforts, catches declined during the 1880's and by the early 1890's it was evident that Arctic whaling was practically exhausted.

In 1893 it was therefore decided to send three ships south to the Antarctic to discover whether the Black Whale was there in sufficient numbers to make it a commercial proposition.

When they returned to Dundee in the spring of 1894, the reports which they brought with them were encouraging and durıng the next twenty years Scottish whaling expeditions regularly sailed to the Antarctic, but the long voyages involved prevented them from ever making large profits and the outbreak of the First World War finally brought these voyages to an end.

After the war it was the Norwegians who completely revolutionised Antarctic whaling by introducing factory ships, and until the late 1950's Scots continued to have a share in the industry through Salvesen's of Leith, until again whaling became uneconomic, because of excessive hunting. Thus today some of the few reminders of the Scottish whaling industry are the carved whales' teeth, giant whales' eardrums and other souvenirs still found in many homes along the shore of the Forth and the Tay.

Chapter 7

From Sealock To Grangemouth

While Scotland's whale oil industry is now only part of history oil is still vitally important in the story of the Forth. For after the First World War when the newly formed Scottish Oils decided to diversify from the production of oil from the shales of West Lothian to the import of oil from the Persian Gulf it was Grangemouth which it chose as its headquarters.

Today Grangemouth is Scotland's only oil refinery and it has grown so rapidly since the end of the Second World War that it is often nicknamed Scotland's Boom Town. Grangemouth could however equally accurately be described as Scotland's Little Holland.

For centuries the Forth ports have all had close links, through trade, with the Low Countries of Europe, and the regular arrival and departure each week of the many small, smartly painted, spotlessly clean Dutch cargo ships is undoubtedly one of the factors which strengthens Grangemouth's resemblance to Holland, but the town has also many physical features which must remind the crews of these vessels of their homeland.

Most important is the flatness of the whole area on which Grangemouth is situated. Admittedly, just across the River Forth the grey Ochil Hills of Fife loom up, but in Grangemouth itself the only suggestions of hills from one end of the town to the other are the artificially created gentle inclines to one or other of the many bridges. As in Amsterdam and other Dutch towns, these numerous bridges are required because of all the narrow waterways, which thread their way through Grangemouth from the outskirts to the centre of the town and on out into the River Forth. Like so many towns in Holland, Grangemouth did, in fact, grow up because of a canal, the thirty-five-mile long Forth and Clyde which, when opened in 1790, was the first

Grangemouth Docks

canal built in Scotland, Until then Grangemouth, or Sealock as it was known at that time, was only a small hamlet of scattered houses, situated unhealthily on the flat marsh ground not far from the black mud flats of the Forth. The choice of Sealock as the eastern terminus of the new canal soon changed all that, for the canal provided Glasgow with a direct water link with the little harbour, and trade soon began to increase. The Glasgow merchants, who had an extensive export trade to the Low Countries, until this time, had to rely on packhorse trains to transport their goods across Central Scotland to the East Coast ports such as Bo'ness. The atrocious roads, rutted and dusty in summer and thick with mud or ice and snow covered in winter, made this a slow and costly journey, which the merchants were delighted to abandon in favour of the comparatively cheap and fast barge transport which the new canal offered. Thus Grangemouth prospered and grew at the expense of its near neighbour, Bo'ness.

When it was begun in 1768 the Forth and Clyde was one of the most ambitious canal projects tackled anywhere in Britain. For along its 35 mile length between the Forth and the Clyde it was necessary to construct 39 locks to raise it to a height of 156 feet (47.5 metres) above sea level. At first digging of the canal progressed swiftly westward from Grangemouth but by the time the work reached Glasgow financial difficulties were encountered and it took a further fifteen years to complete the western portion to Bowling on the Clyde.

For fifty years after that it was one of the busiest transport routes in Scotland, not only for cargo barges, but also for the passenger barges, which until the coming of the railways provided the fastest method of travel between Glasgow and Edinburgh, especially after the completion of the Union Canal, which joined the Forth and Clyde at Port Downie near Falkirk in 1822. From then on so many people chose to travel along this smooth inland waterway, which the Scottish Inland Waterways Association is currently campaigning to reopen as a Trans Scotland Cruiseway, that intending passengers were advised to book in advance at the barge company's headquarters at Port Hamilton near Tollcross. Passengers even had the choice of making the eight hour trip by day during which they could enjoy the delights of the saloon bar and barge restaurant as well as reading books from the barge library and listening to the latest strathspey and reel played by the barge band, or of saving time by travelling by night and sleeping their way across Central Scotland in a comfortable bunk.

The "Hoolets" or "Wee Owls" as the night express barges were affectionately nicknamed sailed each evening at ten from Port Hamilton and Port Dundas and as well as being popular with busy city businessmen, also proved a favourite with young honeymooners.

While the passenger barges were horse drawn the Forth and Clyde Canal was also the scene of several of the earliest experiments into the use of steam power for ship propulsion. As early as 1798 William Symington launched a small steam driven paddle boat on the canal and four years later crowds gathered at Grangemouth to watch his famous Charlotte Dundas, which today forms part of the Stirlingshire burgh's coat of arms. The Charlotte Dundas was a great success, pulling a string of fully laden barges against a strong head wind, but the canal owners banned its use as they feared that its churning stern paddle wheel would cause such a wash that the banks would be damaged.

The coming of steam power could not however be long delayed and eleven years later Henry Bell sailed his black funneled "Comet" from Bowling through the canal to Grangemouth and on down the Forth to the Bo'ness ship building yard of Shaw and Hart, where she was to receive her first annual overhaul.

Yet another claim which the Forth and Clyde Canal has to place in nautical history is that it was on it that the first iron hulled vessel ever constructed in Scotland was launched in 1818. Appropriately named the "Vulcan" she was launched near Falkirk and plied on the canal for many years.

Best remembered and best loved of all the Forth and Clyde fleet of vessels were however the "Fairy Queen" and the "Gypsy Queen", which together carried several generations of Scottish bairns on Sunday school trips and other summer outings. The white hulled "Fairy Queen" continued pleasure sailings on the canal right up to the outbreak of the Second World War in 1939 and advertisements inviting passengers "To sail across Bonny Scotland by Canal" went on to assure them that they would be well provided for the tearoom where they could trip the light fantastic on the minature dance floor to the music of an accordion band.

Today the Forth and Clyde Canal is no longer in use, having closed in 1962, but its towpath still provides an attractive walk, as do the tree-lined banks of the Grange Burn, from which the town took its modern name.

To the west and east two other rivers, the Carron and the Avon, mark the boundaries of the town. Both are tributaries of the Forth and at this point both are sluggish and not at all picturesque. As far as Grangemouth is concerned, the Carron is the more important of the two as it is into muddy waters that the Grangemouth Dockyard Company launches its new ships.

Shipbuilding was one of the many industries which established themselves in Grangemouth during the nineteenth century, and as the town grew more and more land was required. This resulted in yet another similarity with Holland, for just as the Dutch reclaimed the Zuider Zee and other land from the North Sea, so the industrialists of Grangemouth set about reclaiming large areas of the mud flats from the River Forth, and today much of the "New Town" and many of the area's industries stand on land won from the river.

As in Holland, the flatness of the whole area has encouraged many of the workers in these industries to use bicycles to travel to and from work, and as each shift at the giant oil-refinery finishes and as schools close, roads are filled with hordes of cyclists homeward bound. Most now stay in the huge new housing schemes, such as Beancross, and few now pedal home to Grangemouth's Old Town, where the Dutch influence is strongest. Many of the old buildings in this area are at present being demolished, and the huge timber basins in whose still waters they used to be reflected have been filled in. It is a great pity that no Scottish Bruegel captured the scene or that in winter when children delighted in skating on their ice covered surfaces. Today such scenes are only memories but so long as the tulips bloom each spring in the Zetland Park and in the flower beds at Charing Cross, so long as the bookshops of La Porte Precint sell Continental periodicals and Dutch phrase-books, and so long as the town's toilets are signposted "Herrer" as well as "Gentlemen," the Dutch sailors who visit Grangemouth will no doubt continue to find much to remind them of their native land in this, Scotland's "Little Holland".

To construct and open Scotland's largest airport in less than three months would today be considered impossible, but that is what Scottish Aviation undertook and succeeded in doing exactly forty years ago.

Leading lights behind the project were Squadron Leader D. F. McIntyre from Prestwick and Lord Nigel Douglas-Hamilton who together with Mr W. E. Nixon from London, as chairman, and Mr R. L. Angus and Mr T. P. Mills, made up the directors of the newly-formed Scottish Aviation Ltd.

Encouraged by the Maybury Report, which stated that "as the country surrounding both Edinburgh and Glasgow cannot provide individual airports to the required standard in close proximity". Scotland should have one central airport, situated midway between the two cities.

Frantically the directors of Scottish Aviation searched the countryside and decided that the flat farmland on the shores of the River Forth to the south-east of Grangemouth provided the ideal answer. Surprisingly the fact that Scottish Oils Ltd., already had Scotland's only oil refinery on the adjacent site between the flat farmland and the Forth does not appear to have worried Squadron Leader McIntyre and his enthusiastic colleagues.

For the prospectus for the imaginative new venture issued at the beginning of February 1939 they stated: "This piece of land is one of the few in the country where the natural contours assist flying and where man-made obstructions do not exist".

With an optimism which would today appear completely naive they then went on to announce that work would begin on the new aerodrome to be called "Edinburgh Airport" on the following Monday morning and that "one of the most remarkable features of the establishment of this mammoth airport is the fact that contractors have guaranteed to complete the job within three months".

At dawn on Monday, February 6, the contractors arrived on site. Scottish Aviation Ltd., promised the curious public that this was the dawn of a new age for flying in Scotland and the task began of converting the six adjacent farms of Abbotsgrange, Bowhouse, Claret, Reddoch, Dalgleish, Reddock Roy and Wholeflats into the airport.

Amazingly the contractors kept their promise and the imposing grey control tower, passenger terminal buildings and giant aircraft hangers were all completed within three months and were handed over on Thursday, April 29, 1939. The only change from the original prospectus was the name of the airport.

Instead of calling it Edinburgh Airport it was decided that it would more appropriate to call it Scottish Central Airport. Whether this was to avoid petty jealousy with Glasgow or whether it was simply a more accurate geographic description is not explained but instead of changing the first part of the title it would actually have been more appropriate to have changed the second from airport to airfield.

For while the new Central Scotland Airport did indeed have magnificent terminal buildings in the very latest streamlined architectural style of the thirties it did not have one single tarmac runway as even the largest passenger planes were still expected to take off and land on a grass strip.

It was, however, as neither the airport nor the airfield that the people of Grangemouth took the exciting new venture to their hearts, but as the to us nowadays rather quaint "aerodrome" and it was to the "drome," as they quickly nicknamed it, that they flocked in their hundreds on the afternoon of Saturday, May 1, to witness famous air personality Air-Marshall Viscount Trenchard perform the opening ceremony.

An eye-witness, the late Mr Robert Porteous, describes the scene in his history of Grangemouth: "The ceremony which took place in front of the airport buildings was of an unusual nature. Viscount Trenchard started the propellor of a model "Spitfire" aeroplane surmounting a cigar box, which was presented to him and this released a smoke bomb on the grass below the lounge. A moment later a flight of nine Hawker Harts passed over the buildings and flew in formation round the aerodrome, which was circular in shape with a diameter of 1500 yards and was completely surfaced with grass".

The airports's first passenger service was to and from London and it was operated by De Havilland Rapides which could cope with the grass runway and also needed a very short space for take-off.

Ex-Provost of Grangemouth, Lawyer Mr James Burnett White, recalls these early passenger flights: "One of the main additional attractions of Grangemouth as a site was the fact that the aerodrome was only a short distance from Polmont railway station on the main Edinburgh-Glasgow line," he told me. "Many of the passengers travelled out by train and then completed the final mile or two by special coach to the aerodrome. The morning flight to London was timed to coincide with the train timetable".

Sadly, Grangemouth's life as a passenger airport was a very short one because as soon as the Second World War broke out on September 3, 1939, all civilian flights were suspended indefinitely and the aerodrome was taken over by the Air Ministry.

During the war it was used as a training base for fighter pilots not only from the RAF but from all the Commonwealth air forces as well as from Poland. Under the direction of Commanding Officer Group Captain D. V. Carnegie, Gladiators, Blenheims, Lysanders, Whirlwinds, Spitfires and the short-lived Defiants filled the air above Grangemouth and the surrounding Stirlingshire countryside. Towards the end of the war a gliding school was established and it continued into the 1950s.

By the time the air ministry was finished with Grangemouth as a base, it had long been superseded by Turnhouse. and Renfrew and there was no opportunity for it to regain its brief peacetime position as Scotland's main passenger airport. In any case the neighbouring oil refinery had expanded greatly and would have presented an unacceptable hazard. During its war service it had often been affected by fog.

The idea of a central Scotland airport was however revived during the 1960s before the opening of Glasgow Airport, showing just how far before their time Squadron Leader McIntyre and his colleagues had been.

Today the large hangers remain as a last reminder of Grangemouth aerodrome's former glory and local car drivers still motor up the shorter of the two tarred runways built by the Air Ministry during the war years, as it is now the long straight Inchyra Road which make an excellent main link road for all of the housing schemes and industrial estates which now occupy the site where the early forerunner of the shuttle took off.

Grangemouth aerodrome was situated on the banks of the Forth's tributary the Avon. Mention the River Avon and people inevitably assume that you mean the Avon of Stratford and Shakespeare fame, but Scotland too has its River Avon, which rises on Garbethill Muir near Cumbernauld New Town and flows into the Forth midway between Grangemouth and Bo'ness. To begin with this Scottish Avon forms the natural boundary between Central Region and Strathclyde, but it is along its final ten mile stretch as boundary between Stirlingshire and West Lothian that most of the interesting events linked with it took place.

Not far from there it forms West Lothian's western boundary the Avon is joined by its tributary the Brunton Burn and on the shore where they meet is Wallace's Cave, where according to local legend the great Scottish hero found refuge after the Battle of Falkirk. Perhaps the inventor of the first practical steamship, Henry Bell, of "Comet" fame also hid in this cave as a boy, for he was born nearby on the shores of the Avon at Torphichen Mill, which his family worked for many generations. On the Avon, Bell sailed his first little home made toy boats and it was perhaps the river's swift flowing currents whirling his early toys away down stream and out of reach, which first planted in his mind the need for a more effective means of propulsion than sail.

The wooded banks of the Avon were very popular in Victorian times as a spot for family outings and especially Sunday School trips. A special attraction about the banks of the Avon for the Sunday school trippers was that it was possible to travel there from Falkirk and Linlithgow, not by the usual horse drawn brakes or hay carts requisitioned for the day, but by the much more exciting canal barges, which plied on the Union Canal. Highlight of these voyages of adventure of yester year came right at the end of the journey when the bairn laden barges sailed across the impressive twelve arch aquaduct, which carries the canal over the Avon.

Once across the great stone aquaduct the barges tied up and the Sunday school scholars in their stiff Sunday best, clambered down the steep slopes of the Avon Valley to enjoy for an hour or two the freedom of lovely Carribber Glen, where one Rab Gibb built what is known locally as Rab Gibb's castle. An nineteenth century West Lothian author called MacDonald wrote a complete novel called "Stark Love and Kindness" about the almost legendary Rab, but who in actual historic fact he was Jester to King James V, others that he was a stirrup man to the king and yet more that he was merely a servant at the royal palace at Linlithgow, but no matter how lowly his position, he apparantly contrived to make what was in those days a great fortune, which he used to build a large mansion, if not quite the castle as his fellow townsfolk called it.

Gibb certainly choose a beautiful site for his new home and Carribber Glen is still an attractive spot, if somewhat spoiled by the pollution of the Avon, which would have to be greatly improved if the picnic area scheme goes ahead.

Main crossing point on the Avon has always been further down stream at Linlithgow Bridge and it was there that the famous battle of James V's reign took place, when the Earl of Lennox was killed and his army routed by Arran and Angus, while he fought for the infant king's mother.

A modern bridge now carries the main A9, Edinburgh to Stirling road over the river, but the Provost, magistrates and townsfolk of Linlithgow still recall former times, once each year on the first Tuesday after the second Thursday in June, when they ride in procession out to Linlithgow Bridge where the burgh mills once stood, as part of their traditional riding of the marches ceremony.

Some historians also claim that Linlithgow Bridge was the scene of Bothwell's abduction of Mary Queen of Scots, but the more popular view is that this event took place not on West Lothian's western boundary at all, but on the eastern side of the county, where the ill fated Mary was crossing the River Almond.

Further down stream at Inveravon there is another reminder of Scotland's strife torn days in the shape of the ruins of one of the Douglas family's many castles, which was destroyed in 1454 during their feud with James II. Over 1000 years earlier the Romans built a fort on this same site, for it was here that the outermost line of defence of their vast empire, Antonine's Wall, which spanned Scotland from the Forth to the Clyde crossed the Avon.

Inveravon means the mouth or harbour of the Avon and while the Avon today still has some distance to flow, before it meets the Forth, this can be explained because much of the flat land over which it slowly meanders has been reclaimed from the river.

Chapter 8

The Forth At Work

One of the many hills in Bo'ness is still called Tidings Hill, as it was up there that the wives and sweethearts of the whalers used to wait patiently as the days changed from summer into autumn, to catch their first glimpse of the homecoming fleet sailing up river.

The place names Grangepans in Bo'ness and Prestonpans are a lasting reminder of the times when salt-making was Scotland's second most important industry, outrivalled only by coal mining.

Prestonpans means the "priests' pans" and it was in fact monks who began the salt industry in Scotland just as they had earlier been the first to realise the importance of coal.

During the twelfth century the first royal charter for the manufacture of salt was granted by King David I to the monks of Kelso and shortly afterwards the monks of Newbattle Abbey near Dalkeith received a similar charter to set up pans at Prestonpans.

From then on pans were built at points along the Forth as far inland as Kennetpans near Kincardine, wherever coal was readily available close to the shore to provide the necessary fuel. Unlike all of today's salt which is refined from rock salt mined underground, Scottish salt was obtained by boiling sea water until it evaporated, leaving behind the salt as a sparkling white deposit on the bottom of the big shallow black iron pans.

To produce three tons of salt it was necessary to evaporate one hundred tons of water. The task of transferring all the water from the river to the pans was that of the wives and children of the salters, who were "thirled" or bound to the pan at which they laboured.

To lift the water, huge wooden see-saw-like contraptions were built at the water's edge. On one end of the see-saw was fixed a large bucket and this the women and children dipped below the surface. When it was full they pushed with all their might on the other end of the long wooden plank, which raised the bucket into the air, in which position it was then shoved round until it was clear of the river.

The bucket was, never emptied straight into the pan, because even in those days the Forth was not the cleanest of rivers and it was found better to let the water sit in a small reservoir for several days to give the mud and grit a chance to settle.

Even this precaution did not keep all the impurities out of the pan, but once the water was boiling they were removed by emptying a pail of sheep's blood into the steaming solution. The albumen in the blood thickened in the boiling water, forming a scum just like the one that forms on home-made jam and as it rose to the surface it carried with it all the other impurities in the pan. It was then once again the women's unenviable job to lean out over the boiling water and, using long-handled wooden rakes, to skim off the scum, thus leaving the rest of the solution perfectly clear.

The work of evaporating the water then continued day and night. It took fifty tons of coal to produce three tons of salt and the only time that the fires beneath the pans were damped down was on Saturday nights, for the kirk sessions forbade any work on Sundays.

This delay in production was, however, turned to advantage by the wily salt-masters, for the slower rate of evaporation resulted in larger grains of salt being formed and these they marketed as a more expensive table delicacy called "Sabbath salt".

Even the ordinary salt was considered dear by the housewives of the Middle Ages, for the Scottish Parliament cashed in on the fact that it was a vital commodity which every family had to buy in order to keep their meat eatable throughout the winter months and placed a tax on it.

Officially all salt, produced had to be stored in bonded warehouses called "girnels," but the tax resulted in a flourishing salt-smuggling business growing up. The price of salt was also forced up throughout the sixteenth century by the demand for Scottish salt from London, the Low Countries, and Scandinavia.

Salt-making continued along both shores of the Forth throughout the seventeenth and eighteenth centuries, but at the start of the nineteenth century the industry suffered two blows.

The Agricultural Revolution resulted in the introduction of root vegetables for winter fodder, which meant that sheep and cattle could be

kept alive all winter, thus removing the need to salt away mutton and beef. Even worse for the Scottish salt industry was the fact that at the same time salt mines were developed in the North of England and on the Continent.

By 1888 only one of the thirteen pans which had once lit up the night sky at Carriden and acted as a beacon for sailors in the Forth seeking the harbour at Bo'ness was still operating and the fire beneath it was finally allowed to go out in 1890, never to be lit again. But at Joppa and Prestonpans salt for road clearance and for medicinal use continued to be produced until the 1950s.

"They are the best seamen in the Firth and are very good pilots for the Baltic and the coast of Norway." So wrote Daniel Defoe, author of Robinson Crusoe, in the journal of his travels through Scotland, about the sailors of Bo'ness at the beginning of the eighteenth century and ever since then the old West Lothian seaport has maintained strong links with the Scandinavian countries.

Regatta Day, Bo'ness

Lying as it does on the southern shore of the River Forth and built on a series of what geologists describe as raised beaches, which rise like the tiers of an enormous wedding cake above the well-filled bottom layer containing the old harbour with its warehouses and quayside inns, Bo'ness resembles many of the Norwegian coastal towns.

Sailing up the Forth, the resemblance is even more marked as the Enrgath Hills with their wooded slopes rise behind the town, but unfortunately it is no longer possible to approach Bo'ness from the river, except in the smallest pleasure craft, because its once bustling harbour and dock were closed down almost ten years ago as an ecomomy move by the British Transport Commission. It was, however, by sea that the town's links with Norway were first forged, for as early as the fifteenth century Bo'ness had a thriving export trade in both coal and salt to the Scandinavian lands.

By the nineteenth century the balance of trade had swung in the opposite direction with the main trade at Bo'ness being the import of Baltic timber, mainly for use in the large number of coal pits in the area. The demand for wood from the mining industry increased enormously just over a hundred years ago, when Scottish pits changed over from the

Bo'ness Dock with its coal hoists and crane.

traditional stoop and room method of working to the new and much more efficient longwall system. Using the old stoop and room method the miners had to leave large stoops or pillars of coal at frequent intervals to hold up the roof of the tunnel, but from about 1840 onwards all this waste was done away with as the longwall system gained popularity. The longwall system meant that the whole length of the seam was worked with timber supports replacing the coal stoops. To begin with, full length tree trunks were imported and at the beginning of each shift the miners had to saw up the number of props of various sizes, which they reckoned they would require during the day. This method was very wasteful, because the miners never bothered about making the best use of each tree and many short lengths of timber were often left over, quite possibly deliberately, as the miners were allowed to collect the scrap and take it home to burn on their fires.

This continual waste was noticed by the cashier at the Grange Colliery, Bo'ness, Mr George C. Stewart. The Grange Colliery was at that time owned by the Cadell family of the Grange, and Mr Stewart's astuteness was later described by Mr Henry M. Cadell in his book, *The Rocks of the Forth.* Mr Stewart's idea was simply to import the pit props at regular intervals in a variety of sizes, lengths and diameters, and these he supplied ready for use to all the pits in the Bo'ness area. To do this he went into partnership with a Glasgow business man, Mr James Love, and together they set up the first pit wood yard at Bo'ness, in an area of flat ground which had recently been reclaimed from the

River Forth. The success of the new venture was immediate and it soon expanded. Other rival firms were set up and in 1881 the old North British Railway Company built a large new dock at Bo'ness to meet the needs of the new trade.

Bo'ness was rapidly surrounded by a forest of pit props piled high in yard after yard, stretching all the way along the foreshore to the Forth from Kinneil in the west, down river to Carriden in the east.

The founder of the pit prop industry, Mr George Stewart, became one of the most successful business men in Bo'ness, and was for many years the town's provost. During his term in office he did much to improve Bo'ness by bringing about the widening of the narrow winding streets, the provision of a better water supply and the opening of a new public park, but he will always be especially remembered for the work which he did to transform the town's fair day from a drunken miners' orgy into the spectacular children's day which always brings thousands of exiled Bo'nessians back to their home town for one magic day each summer.

By the time Provost Stewart retired from business, his firm and the other Bo'ness pitwood companies had extended their interests by setting

up new prop yards at Grangemouth, South Alloa, Portobello, Granton and other seaport town both in Scotland and the North of England to serve the various mining areas. To begin with, the Scottish firms bought individual cargoes of spruce and fir from forestry owners in Norway, Sweden, Finland and Russia, but before long they, themselves, purchased large forests in many parts of Scandinavia so that they could control their raw material from the source. Several of them also acquired their own ships, such as Love and Stewart's *Lovart,* to transport the pit props to the Forth, and the "prop" boats, laden with their heavy deck cargoes, became a familiar sight as they anchored in the roads off Bo'ness and Grangemouth awaiting the tide or queueing for berths in the docks.

Importing pit wood had its hazards, and the small cargo ships engaged in this trade often took a fierce battering from the North Sea gales. Loss of sections of deck cargo was not infrequent and several of the pit prop boats never reached harbour. One of the most famous wrecks was the S. S. *Skoghaugh,* which was driven ashore on the coast

Sunday afternoon?

near Dunbar. As the crew battled to save their ship they jettisoned much of the deck cargo. Many of the pit props were salvaged by local fishermen while others were later washed ashore further south near Cockburnspath.

During the war a number of the "prop" boats were torpedoed and several of these casualties limped into Scottish ports, but these were the only cargoes of pit wood landed in Scotland between 1939 and 1945. For Scotland, during the war, for the first time supplied all her pit prop requirements from the home forests. This effort, however placed an unexpectedly heavy demand on home-grown timber and soon after peace was declared in 1945 the import of pit props began again. In the first cargoes the workers in the Scottish yards found many interesting souvenirs of the fighting in Norway and the Baltic Countries in the form of bullets and shattered shell tips which were embedded in the timber a grim reminder of the German occupation which this country had so narrowly escaped.

After the war some cargoes of pit props were obtained from Portugal, which supplied them to us in return for coal. All the time, however, Scotland's forests in Argyllshire, Perthshire and other areas were being carefully redeveloped and greatly extended until during the 1950's the need to import foreign pit props grew less and less as home-grown timber became available in ever increasing amounts.

The prop trade will always be remembered in Bo'ness for it led to one of the most colourful incidents in the town history.

The Battle of Slaghill is not mentioned in any Scottish history book, but ask any old age pensioners who linger on the street corners in Bo'ness they will still tell you of the quiet May day in 1910 when violence suddenly flared in the old West Lothian seaport town.

Every spring when the Baltic ice melted, the heavily laden prop boats with their deck cargoes began to arrive at Bo'ness Dock, bringing pit wood for collieries all over Scotland from Norway, Sweden, Russia, and Finland.

In the spring of 1910, however, the prop boats did not receive their usual welcome from the townsfolk, because there was seething discontent in the pit wood yards over a wage cut which the employers had forced on the men under the excuse of depression in the trade.

Instead of 6d on hour, the labourers were being paid only 5d and their anger increased when they heard that workers in propyards of the neighbouring ports of Grangemouth and Alloa were still being paid at the old rate.

Through the union which they had recently formed, the men asked their employers to pay them the extra penny again, but they were met with a steadfast refusal even to consider it.

Finally, at the end of May all the prop workers came out on strike—and the battle for the penny, the Battle of Slaghill began.

Rumours immediately spread through Bo'ness that the prop yard owners intended to break the strike early the next morning by hiring hundreds of blacklegs from Glasgow where there were plenty of men unemployed.

A strong force of police was already on guard long before the special train bringing the Glasgow workers came into sight, steaming down the single-line track from Manuel Junction shortly before six a.m.

Jeers and shouts greeted the incomers, but they were allowed to proceed unmollested into the prop yards where they soon started stacking the pit props.

It looked indeed as if the extra policemen had been called out unnecessarily as the strikers made their way back along Corbiehall, as one of the main streets in the town is still called, into the centre of Bo'ness.

This was, however, only a temporary lull for the strikers had merely returned to the town to gather reinforcements. For the next three hours they marched back and forth through the winding, cobbled streets.

As news of the forth-coming battle spread, they were joined by several hundred foundry workers who stopped work for the day to support the propyard men.

Inside the propyard, the Glasgow men watched anxiously. As the first ranks of strikers advanced upon them, the constables drew their truncheons. For a second the strikers halted, then urged on by the shouts of their women folk, they let fly a hail of stones and charged the police.

The police stood no chance and were swiftly swept aside. As they entered the yard each striker grabbed a pit prop. The Battle of Slaghill had begun.

All over the yard skirmishes began as the Bo'ness workers fell upon the Glaswegians. Seeing that they were outnumbered many of the Glasgow men did not wait to fight but tried to hide under the long lines

of railway waggons and in the yard bothies.

Relentlessly the Bo'nessians hunted them down and despite the pleas for mercy, battered them with the heavy pit props.

As the battle raged the yard clerks, who had not stopped work along with the men, barricaded themselves in their office. But the strikers were not interested in them. They wanted the blood of the Glasgow invaders.

Suddenly they heard that a group of Glasgow men were hiding between two of the long high lines of stacks of pit props.

The incomers could not have picked a worse refuge and well the strikers knew it, for the far end of the narrow gap was blocked by another huge stack of props and once in there was no way out . . . "a veritable Khyber Pass" wrote one of the reporters who covered the battle from the front line.

Led by their leader, nicknamed "Showman Bill," one group of strikers guarded the entrance to the narrow defile while the others climbed up on top of the piles of props and pushed down the heavy round pieces of wood on top of the terrified blacklegs. As the avalanche of tree trunks rushed down on them the trapped men yelled their surrender and were dragged out by the victorious Bo'ness men.

In other parts of the yard, the battle continued with fierce bursts of fighting as group after group of the enemy were ferreted out of their hiding places.

Some of the Glasgow men tried desperately to escape by fleeing out of the far side of the yard on the shores of the Forth, but they found themselves cut off by the river.

Mercilessly they were pursued out onto the oozing black mudflats, where the fight continued. Others found themselves trapped on the steep crumbling slopes of the Slaghill coal bing.

Just as the battle looked like turning into a massacre, the employers announced that they would meet the strikers' representatives and try to reach a settlement.

As quickly as they had entered the yard, the Bo'ness men withdrew and marched triumphantly back into the town, leaving behind them a trail of havoc among the prop stacks and over fifty seriously injured Glasgow men. Another 200 suffered minor bruises.

As one of the prop yard clerks, young Fred Farquharson noted down their names and the extent of their injuries, the local G.P., Doctor Fischer, made the Glasgow strike breakers as comfortable as possible before they were helped back to the special train.

When it left, after one p.m., many Glaswegians could not be found, but they later boarded the train four miles away at Polmont Junction to which they had run and walked across the fields, rather than remain any longer in Bo'ness.

As soon as the train arrived back in Glasgow, the injured men were rushed to Glasgow Infirmary for treatment for injuries ranging from broken arms to concussion.

The injuries resulted in a series of compensation cases being brought against the Bo'ness pit prop yard owners, whose summons had in the first place involved them in the Battle of Slaghill.

After three months of negotiations during the summer, the strikers were awarded their pay rise. It was a bitter disappointment to them for they were eventually awarded half of what they asked for.

Pitprops, coal, oil and salt all combined at one time to make Bo'ness second only to Leith among Scotland's seaports, a fact recognised by Customs officers, who looked upon it as promotion to transferred to Bo'ness from Glasgow.

However, just as in the eighteenth century, Bo'ness won its trade from Blackness, three miles down river, so during the last one hundred years it gradually lost it all again to superior port facilities five miles up river at Grangemouth.

Bo'ness has, however, retained several links with its sea-going past, one of the most interesting of which is the town's Sea Box Society. The society takes its name from the iron-bound sea chest into which the Bo'ness skippers used to put one-tenth of their profits from every

Bo'ness en fete on a Fair Day

successful voyage to provide the town with its own seventeenth century version of the modern welfare state.

Similar friendly societies were established in many other Scottish towns, but apart from one in Aberdeen, the Borrowstounness General United Sea Box was the oldest in the country. Its centuries-old records are still all in existence and they state that it was through the diligence of a number of the town's sea captains that the Sea Box was founded in 1634, "for benevolent purposes, and for mutual help in times of need".

When they returned to Bo'ness after every successful voyage captains gave a proportion of their profits to the Sea Box, which received its name from the fact that all the money was kept in a large box or chest, strengthened with bands of iron and with a massive lock.

Every month a meeting of the members was held in order to decide how the funds should be used and there was a strict rule that money must never be taken out of the box unless at least two ships' masters were present.

A careful note was also kept of all the uses to which the funds were put

Early "Fair Day" Arch at the Snab

and the Sea Box's records are full of entries detailing the granting of pensions to old sailors or their widows, the allocation of allowances to children whose fathers had been lost at sea, and the payment of sickness benefits.

Some of the entries are however far from routine. Against the date April 7, 1749, for instance is noted: "Given to James Campbell taken by the Algerians in a vessel called the Swallow. After three years' slavery released by a Maltese ship of war".

Slavery was apparently by no means the worst fate which could befall Scottish sailors who were unlucky enough to be captured by the Algerians, for one year later appears the following grim entry. "To William McPharson and two others whose tongues were cut out by the Turks of Algiers. All three in a melancholy state."

Apart from Bo'ness sailors the Sea Box also appears to have been generous to foreign seamen who were shipwrecked in Scotland or for some other reason needed money. For instance, one entry for February 7, 1704, reads: "Given to a shipbroken Dutchman by order," while another reads, "Given to five poore Frenchmen of St Maloos, taken by the Ostenders".

Bo'ness in days gone by

Bo'ness was at that time Scotland's second most important seaport and one result of this prosperity was that the ships' masters and other members of the Sea Box frequently did not claim the benefits to which they were entitled, leaving them for their less well off fellow townsfolk.

Even when all the needy had been provided for, a considerable sum of money always remained in the big sea chest, until the sea captains all agreed that there was far too much simply to hoard it away. They therefore decided to make the funds work for them by investing the money and the records note several sums entrusted to captains who were bound for Holland, where they were instructed to invest the money as profitably as possible with the rich Continental merchants.

The Scottish skippers obviously placed the Sea Box's money very wisely, because it was soon rich enough to be in a position to lend money to no less a person than the Duke of Hamilton, who owned most of the land and property around Bo'ness. As it prospered the Sea Box also bought land for itself and built houses.

Apart from members' payments, rents from its properties, and profits

Old Bo'ness

from its investments, more money came into the old Sea Box from the society's right to charge dues on all the gangways and barrows used to unload both cargo vessels and fishing boats at Bo'ness harbour.

This was only one of several privileges which the Sea Box gained, another being the right to appoint the town bellman. Once an enterprising young man in the town tried to challenge this monopoly to make public announcements by setting himself up as a rival town crier, using a horn instead of a bell to attract attention.

Immediately alive to this threat to its bellman's livelihood, the Sea Box appealed to the Court at Linlithgow, but before the case could be heard the interloper gave in.

At one time the Sea Box Society even owned a mortcloth which was lent out in those days when coffins were an expense few families in Bo'ness could afford. Now the mortcloth is no longer required and the other friendly society activities of the Sea Box have been largely superseded by the provisions of the welfare state, but it still survives and membership is a right carefully guarded by many Bo'ness families.

Meetings of members are held regularly in the society's own hall where the original sea chest still occupies pride of place. There too can

Summer Regatta off Bo'ness

be seen its old hand bell, which was last rung at the close of the town's tercentenary exhibition, held in 1968 to mark the three-hundreth anniversary of Bo'ness's becoming a burgh, three hundred years during which the Sea Box itself helped to shape much of the old seaport's history.

Bridgeness once a port in its own right today maintains the last active but rather sad link which Bo'ness has with shipping, for it is there that — Daltons, formerly P & W. McLellan Ltd., have their shipbreaking yard.

Sad though it undoubtedly is to watch a vessel completing her last voyage, it is nonetheless a very impressive sight to see a ship arriving to be broken up at Bridgeness. Unlike the procedure at the shipbreakers at Faslane in the Gareloch, or at Inverkeithing further down the Forth it is not a simple matter of the old ship slipping quietly alongside the quay.

At Bo'ness it involves a great deal more excitement, as the old liner or naval vessel swings round out in the middle of the Forth until exactly in

line with the tall breaker's crane. Then the order "full speed ahead" is given, and the ship races for the shore in a magnificent last suicidal rush.

For a moment it looks as if she must career on into the cottages which line the shore road, then suddenly there is a tremendous crash as she grounds fast, usually only feet from the spot marked out for her in the breaker's yard, thanks to the skill of Bo'nessian Jackie Findlater and his fellow Forth pilots, who have performed this difficult operation on many occasions, often with the complete ship's crew still on board.

Even taller than the shipbreaking yard crane at Bridgeness is Bridgeness Tower. The tower stands on the site of the eastern end of Antonine's Wall, the Romans' outermost line of defence, which stretched across Central Scotland to Bowling on the Clyde. But the tower was not, as many people think, erected as a memorial to the many Roman legionaries and their auxiliaries who came reluctantly from warm sunny Italy to cold windy Bo'ness to defend their empire against the Picts.

Bridgeness Tower was in fact originally built as one of Scotland's few windmills, to provide power to work the pumps needed to remove the water which constantly flooded into the coal pits, whose workings ran right out under the bed of the river.

The tower's use as a windmill was however short-lived, because the

Cadells of Grange, who owned all the collieries, were forward-looking industrialists and they decided to invest in one of the new steam engines, which became available at the end of the eighteenth century.

For a time the old windmill stood unused until the early years of nineteenth century when it was rented by an English industrialist called Hughes, who had come to Bo'ness to set up what the local people called the "Secret Factory".

The factory earned its name because the Bo'nessians regarded Mr Hughes as a kind of wizard who, working behind the high walls and closed gates of his factory, produced a strange liquid which was as clear as water yet could burn like fire.

This was oil of vitriol, or sulphuric acid as we know it. But to the townsfolk of Bo'ness it was not far short of a miracle. They were not very surprised therefore, when Mr Hughes rented Bridgeness Tower and announced that he was going to establish an observatory so that he could study the heavens.

Before long the huge sails were stripped from the tower and the mill machinery was removed, but even Mr Hughes's scientific knowledge could not solve the intricacies of putting together the £1,000 six-inch telescope which he had brought north in parts from London. In the end he hired an English astronomer called Clarke to come to Bo'ness to assemble the telescope and show him how to use it.

According to his original contract Clarke was to stay at Bridgeness Tower for only six months, but he eventually stayed for almost thirty years and during that time became one of the town's most colourful characters.

From a day early on his stay at the Tower, when his servant carelessly lost a half-sovereign, he insisted on doing his own shopping. On these daily excursions he always wore a tall silk hat, which made him a figure of great interest to the Bo'ness children, who believed that in some strange way this peculiar man from the tower controlled the weather.

"What kind of day will it be the morn?" they always yelled when he appeared, and he always had an answer for them.

On Sundays, Mr Clarke did not stroll into Bo'ness. Instead he went in the other direction from the tower along the shore of the Forth to nearby Carriden Church, where his burst of laughter frequently interrupted the minister even during the prayers.

When Mr Hughes died, his telescope was removed from the tower and sold to the Astronomer Royal. The tower's four large round rooms were then converted into houses, which were inhabited until the 1950's.

Today another local character very popular with the Bo'ness children stays just below Bridgeness Tower in attractively named "Floral Cottage". He is Mr James Cuthell, who until his retirement had been musical director at every Bo'ness Children's Fair Festival since the Second World War.

Starting with the revival of the Fair—the largest event of its kind in the country—in 1946. Mr Cuthell conducted the bands and massed choir of more than three thousand schoolchildren at every Fair until laying down his baton for the last time with the coronation of "queen,"

The author with the present Dr John Roebuck, when he presented him with the Quarter Plate from H.M.S. Roebuck, prior to the deliberate sinking of the vessel during a naval gunnery practice in the Forth. Dr Roebuck's wife and sons were also present for the ceremony at the southern end of the Forth Road Bridge.

Jean Dewar on 30th June, 1972.

Mr Cuthell's last year as the town's musical director was fittingly marked by a visit from the BBC television programme,"Songs of Praise," and for it Mr Cuthell had the honour of conducting a combined choir of adults and children from all the other choirs in Bo'ness.

The service was televised from beautiful Carriden Church, with its old carved wooden sailing ship sailing high above the pews, that Mr Cuthell taught his son Tom, to play the organ.

Today Tom, a former assistant at St Giles' in Edinburgh, is the lively young minister of the city's historic St Cuthbert's Parish Church.

Carriden Church is surrounded by the ruins of the older parish church and many centuries-old tombstones, among the most interesting of which is that of Dr John Roebuck. Inscribed in Latin upon it are the words, "Underneath this tombstone rests no ordinary man, John Roebuck, MD".

Every Scot has heard of James Watt and the important

improvements which he made to the steam engine, but few know much about Dr John Roebuck, the industrialist who had the vision to encourage and finance his experiments. Yet it was this enterprising Englishman who really started the Industrial Revolution in Scotland.

Born in 1718, Dr Roebuck was the son of a prosperous Sheffield cutler, but despite his proven ability at school and his father's wealth he could not go to either Oxford or Cambridge, England's only two universities in the eighteenth century, because of the Religious Test Act, which insisted that all students must be communicants of the Church of England, while he was a Nonconformist.

Scotland had no Test Act and so the young Roebuck came north for the first time to study medicine at Edinburgh University. Later to complete his studies he travelled to what was then the world's leading medical school at Leyden in Holland, but when it came time for him to practise he discovered that he was after all not cut out to be a doctor, as he could not stand the sufferings unavoidably inflicted upon patients in these days long before the discovery of anaesthetics and antiseptics.

He therefore turned to his second love, the study of metals, and decided to set up his own factory, where he could put his researches into practice.

Seeking a suitable site, he remembered the lonely shore of the Forth near Prestonpans where he had once wandered during his student days in Edinburgh, and it was there that he set up the works where he perfected the lead chamber method of producing sulphuric acid.

Dr Roebuck's Prestonpans factory soon became the largest producer of the acid in Britain and it was while enjoying this success that he was approached by a business man from neighbouring Cockenzie, Mr William Cadell, with a proposal for a much more ambitious venture, Mr Cadell was a member of a well-to-do East Lothian merchant family whose main business was the import of iron from Russia and Sweden.

At the time the Seven Years' War was increasing the demand for iron, for making cannon and other weapons, but the hostilities were at the same time disrupting the supply from the Swedish and Russian ore mines. Mr Cadell therefore suggested to Dr Roebuck that the time was ripe to exploit the large quantities of ironstone, which he was certain existed in Scotland, and that they should build Scotland's first large iron works.

Always eager for a new challenge Dr Roebuck immediately agreed to the scheme and spent the whole spring and summer of 1759 using his knowledge of metallurgy to discover the richest source of ironstone, which was eventually located near Bo'ness, the old West Lothian mining and seaport town on the south shore of the river Forth.

When it came to the choice of a site for the new works Roebuck was as careful as he had been over selection of the source of its raw material. Unlike his partner, Mr Cadell, who had given the matter no greater thought than to consider that the works should be sited as near as possible to his home in East Lothian. Dr Roebuck was at pains to explain that the choice of location could make all the difference between the success and failure of the venture.

The doctor considered that the works must be built within easy reach of the seams of ironstone at Bo'ness and yet be as close as possible to the Highland forests, for charcoal was still considered essential to smelt the iron. An adequate water supply was also necessary, while sea transport for the finished products would be a decided advantage.

In the end the excellent and now famous site at Carron near Falkirk was chosen. With a sense of timing and ceremony which would delight the modern public relations man, the factory was opened at dawn on New Year's Day 1760.

The giant water wheel, bellows, and air furnaces, which were considered among the engineering wonders of the age, had all been started the night before and by dawn all was ready for Dr Roebuck to draw off the first molten metal and pour it into a mould in front of the guests who had been invited to watch the proceedings. Scottish historians agree that this marked the start of the Industrial Revolution in Scotland, as from then on the country had the iron to make the new machines and other products which were to change its whole way of life.

To ensure the supply of ironstone for Carron, Dr Roebuck leased from the Duke of Hamilton the Bo'ness coalfield, in which the bands of ironstone were found, and at the same time also rented Kinneil House, the Bo'ness home of the Duke of Hamilton, which still stands high on a hill overlooking the river Forth.

It was the river which soon began to cause Roebuck continual trouble as it flooded into the pit workings, most of which ran out under its bed. It was this problem which first brought him into contact with James Watt.

Dr Roebuck had already installed a Newcomen steam engine to work the pumps, but the English inventor's machine could not cope with the huge inrushes of water. His interest was therefore immediately aroused when his friend Professor Black of Glasgow University told him about the experiments being carried out by the young James Watt to increase the efficiency of the steam engine by introducing the condenser.

Watt was soon invited to visit Roebuck at Kinneil, but from the outset he showed the lack of haste and seeming lack of enthusiasm which ran through their whole relationship. At first he pleaded that his health was too poor to allow him to undertake the journey from Glasgow to Kinneil, but since it was just over twenty-five miles this seems to have been simply an excuse. Watt was in the middle of one of his periods of depression and doubt about his experiments.

However, after Dr Roebuck gave Watt £1,000 to clear his debts and, even more important, a great amount of encouragement to go on with his work, the inventor came to stay at Kinneil and began work in top secrecy in the little workshop, the ruins of which can still be seen behind the big house.

When Watt's work progressed beyond the models, which he displayed to Roebuck on the big dining-room table, and he was ready to build his first full-scale engine the doctor arranged to have the parts made at Carron. But when they arrived they were so inaccurate that there was a steady loss of steam.

At this point, according to Roebuck family legend, it was the doctor who came to the rescue. For as he watched the steam putting out he suddenly whipped off one of his top boots, cut off a ring from round the top, and rammed it down between the cylinder and the piston, thus inventing the first steam packing.

Even Dr Roebuck's ingenuity could not increase the efficiency of Watt's new engine sufficiently to enable it to rid the Burn Pit of water when it was finally installed in 1769. In the end the flooding problem forced him to sell his shares in Carron and give up his lease of the pits in order to pay off his debts, while his two-third share of the patent for Watt's engine, which by then was looked upon as a white elephant, was transferred to Matthew Boulton, the Birmingham industrialist.

The remainder of the story of how the better-made English components made all the difference to the efficiency of Watt's engine, and of how he was encouraged to go ahead and adapt it to rotary motion, is well-known, but what is not nearly so well-known is that his

Wedding Jugs and a Surprise Mug from Marshall's Pottery, Bo'ness.

former Scottish partner, Dr John Roebuck, survived his financial crisis and went on to found Scotland's first large commercial pottery.

With all his old enthusiasm the doctor set about planning his new enterprise, which had been wisely chosen to utilise the local resources of cheap coal for the kiln fires, cheap female labour, and the availability of the river Forth to transport the raw materials and easily breakable finished products, which was a vital consideration in those days when Scotland's roads were still bumpy, rutted dust bowls in summer and muddy quagmires in winter.

Some clay was available locally, but most was imported from Devon and Cornwall, along with flints from France and large grinding stones from the West of Scotland, all of which were unloaded straight from the sailing ships that brought them up the Forth into the pottery, strategically sited on the bank of the river at Bridgeness near Bo'ness.

The pottery proved a huge success, but it was not, unfortunately, until after Roebuck's death in 1794 that it really became profitable.

During his many years in residence at Kinneil Roebuck did a great

deal to improve Bo'ness, including the provision of its first fresh water supply, the improvement of roads, and the deepening and extension of the town's harbour. It was in the town of his adoption that the remarkable doctor was finally buried.

His grave is in Carriden Parish Churchyard, within sight of the river Forth, the river which flowed right through his life from the time he started his first secret factory at Prestonpans until he launched his last venture at Bridgeness.

The inscription on his marble tombstone begins, "Under this tombstone rests no ordinary man, John Roebuck, M.D.," and ends, "The magnificent work at the mouth of the Carron is his own invention".

Chapter 9

Ship Shape and Blackness Fashion

With Scottish oil interests to guard out in the North Sea, will one of the Scottish National Party's demands ever be a Scottish Navy? One admiral who wanted this a century ago was Admiral Sir James Hope.

Sir James was born in 1808 at Carriden House, which still stands high on a hill overlooking the River Forth, on the outskirts of Bo'ness. His father, Admiral Sir George Hope, who was Commander-in-Chief of the British Fleet in the Baltic during the Napoleonic Wars and was in command of HMS Defence at the Battle of Trafalgar, died when young James was only ten, but by that time he had imbued his son with his own love of the sea.

Eager to follow in his father's distinguished wake, James joined the Navy when he was fifteen, and by 1838 he had reached the rank of captain. While captain of the Firebrand he officially opened the River Parana in South America to navigation. Later, during Britain's war with China, he was appointed commander-in-chief in the Far East, and his greatest success was the capture of Peking.

With the great Scottish regiments in mind, Admiral Hope constantly pressed the Admiralty in London to create Scottish ships of the line with Scottish names and manned entirely by Scottish sailors.

Even without the Admiralty's blessing for this scheme, the Admiral contrived to make up a large part of his own ship's company from Scots. Many of the men were from his own home area of Carriden and Bo'ness and they were only too eager to serve under Hope, because he was extremely popular and had a reputation for fairness in those days when Naval discipline was still often harsh.

Hope's loyalty to his home town paid off in dramatic fashion on one occasion during the China campaign, when a Bo'ness sailor called Tom Grant saved his life by knocking him clear a split second before an enemy shell struck the deck where he had been standing.

Throughout his naval career, Admiral Hope was convinced that Scottish sailors' loyalty to their ships would be increased still further if they had their own distinctive Scottish uniform and the Admiralty did allow him to experiment with this idea, which included tartan balmorals.

The Scottish uniform unfortunately did not prove very popular, but one of the Admiral's Scottish ideas which did was his encouragement of the production of Scottish plays aboard ship. This he did by transforming the main deck of his warship into a makeshift theatre, where with the Admiral himself as producer rehearsals provided a welcome diversion during long days at sea.

When all was ready the officers and crews of other vessels in the fleet were invited aboard to see these Scottish shows, the most successful of which proved to be "Rob Roy," because, as the Admiral later wrote: "It provided plenty of action and fights, both for my men who played all the parts and for the sailors who made up the audience."

When he retired from the Navy, Admiral Hope showed to the people of Carriden, who stayed near his home, the same interest which he had displayed towards his ship's company. One of his most successful efforts was the creation of a model village which still stands grouped neatly round the crossroads at Muirhouses.

Apart from cottages, the village included a school where the Admiral's sister instructed the local girls in the art of needlework and although the school has long been closed, the school room has recently been given a new lease of life by a local couple, John and Mary Doherty, who have started their own little clothing industry, which would no doubt have delighted the old Admiral, for it is producing high-quality tartan products, which find a ready sale on the export market. This has now proved so successful that it has expanded to a full scale factory in the new town of Cumbernauld.

Carriden also has a military link, for it was there that Colonel James Cardiner, whom Scott makes Edward Waverley's commanding officer at the Battle of Prestonpans, was born in 1687.

Two miles farther down river, set high on a hill overlooking the whole of the Firth, the turreted Binns House was the home of an even more famous, or infamous, Scottish soldier, General Tam Dalyell, who persecuted the Covenanters with such vigour that they nicknamed him "Bloody Dalyell".

It is claimed that the Binns which is Gaelic for hills has been dwelt in ever since Pictish times. To this day, in fact, legend has it that one of the Picts lingers on in the shape of the ghostly figure of a small man clad all in brown, who haunts the two hills from which the Binns takes its name.

Tradition relates that the Picts always build on rock and an outcrop of rock does occur beneath the stone-flagged kitchen floor of the Binns, for whose fire the little old Pict is said to gather wood.

Nor is the wee Pict the only ghostly resident, for the pond by the main gate is alleged to be the home of a water sprite, while the hillock by the old entrance known as the Black Lodge on the main Queensferry to Bo'ness Road has always been known as the home of a spirit who in Victorian times often caused horses to bolt.

The most famous of the Binns ghosts is, however, very appropriately its most famous occupier General Tam Dalyell, or "Bluidy Tam" as he was more often known to the Covenanters, whom he tracked down with a ruthless efficiency.

Now almost three centuries after his death the wily General is said still to return to the Binns by night and mounted on a ghostly white charger gallops across the ruined bridge over the Errack Burn and up the winding road to his old home.

While the Covenanters believed that the Devil laid a spell on General

Tam so that their bullets could not harm him and were convinced that the Devil carefully instructed him on especially painful means with which to torture them, other stories maintain that the De'il and Dalyell were not on nearly such good terms and that indeed they frequently quarrelled.

After one particularly bitter row the Devil warned Dalyell: "I will blow down your house on top of you". Believing that actions spoke louder than words Dalyell promptly summoned his estate workers and hurriedly built protective walls. When they were complete the Devil returned, eyed them up and down and declared: "Now I'll just have to huff harder and blow down your house and your guid new walls."

"Oh no you won't," retorted Dalyell, "for I'll build me a turret at every corner to pin down my walls," and to this day there are still walls and at every corner turrets which serve no apparent useful purpose.

This was not General Tam's only victory over Auld Nick for on another occasion he succeeded in beating the Devil at cards. Mad with rage the Devil seized the marble topped card table and hurled it at Dalyell's head. The general ducked and the massive table top hurtled on to plunge into the dark waters of the kelpie's pool.

The story of the Devil's gambling defeat could well be dismissed as a tall tale, but today, visitors to the Binns, can see the carved table top, for a century ago during a particularly dry summer the troopers of the Scots Greys while watering their famous grey horses found the marble slab embedded in the mud and dragged it back up to the house.

It was particularly appropriate that the soldiers of the Greys should find the general's table, for it was Dalyell who first raised their standard at the Binns in 1681. Frustrated at the Covenanters frequently escaping his grasp as their lookouts could all too easily spot the scarlet jackets of his Redcoats, he sent a special order to Holland for bales of grey cloth to be made into uniforms.

It was from them and not from the grey horses which they later rode to glory at the Battle of Waterloo that they took their name.

Officers and men of the Scots Greys Dragoon Guards in uniform still have the privilege of free entry to the Binns, but while they have long abandoned their horses for armoured cars, the other creatures traditionally associated with the old house — the famous Binns peacocks — still strut proudly through the grounds as if well aware of the importance which is attached to them. For just like the apes on the

Rock of Gibraltar being accepted as a guarantee that it will remain British so legend has it that so long as the peacocks parade proudly on the lawns of the Binns so will it remain in the hands of the Dalyell family.

Legend also maintains that there is a hidden secret passage linking the house with Blackness Castle.

Even without a secret tunnel the approach to Blackness is an exciting one. The massive iron yett of the castle meets visitors when they arrive after driving out along the long promontory of volcanic rock from which this dramatically situated castle on the shores of the Forth takes its name.

Inside the gate, the narrow confines are skilfully constructed. Part of the entrance is sharply right angled. In the days before cannon were invented these sudden turns gave Blackness protection against the use of battering rams, while each bend gave the defenders a position to fall back to in the unlikely event of the yett being forced.

One question which is most intriguing about the riverside fort is why is it so appropriately shaped like an ancient sailing ship with its bows jutting out into the Firth as if ready to cast off?

Most delightful of the answers is the story that King James V appointed Archibald Douglas to be Lord High Admiral of the Scottish Fleet, only to discover that Douglas was violently sea sick whenever he put to sea. Involved in the customary battles against the English, King James was eager that his navy should be as active as possible in attacking the enemy and therefore proposed to dismiss Douglas and replace him with a true sailor. Douglas however desperately wished to retain his command as selling positions in the navy was a money spinning proposition and he therefore tried to persuade the king that he was indeed a competent admiral by promising to equip the Scottish navy with "a ship that would never sink".

Blackness was the result, but most historians believe that it was the nature of the site, and not any thought out plan which gave Blackness its unique design. But no matter Blackness Castle is certainly "ship-shape". From the waves crashing against the fo'csle the battlements stretch aft to form the bulwarks of this great stone man o' war, complete with its tall Main Mast Tower and its lofty stern tower, which just as on a sailing ship of the Middle Ages, contained the captain's, or governor's, quarters.

Blackness has probably been a fortified site ever since Roman galleys berthed in the bay to supply the auxiliaries hard at work on Antonine's Wall, which began a short distance up river at Bridgeness, but the present castle was most likely begun by the De Vipont family to defend their estate of Carriden.

In the middle of the fourteenth century the De Viponts lost their lands to the Crown, but the next written record about the castle describes it as being in the hands of the Douglas family, who in the reign of James II, menaced the power of the throne. This threat as far as Blackness was concerned was ended in 1743 when the castle was seized from the Douglases by Chancellor Crichton, Governor of Stirling Castle.

This, in turn, led to one of the most intriguing incidents in the history of the castle, when instead of leaving Blackness in his will to his eldest son, old Crichton left it to the king. The son refused to be robbed of his prize and imprisoned his father in the castle and threatened to defy the king.

James could not let this go unchallenged and in 1453 began the most famous siege of Blackness, which included the use of ships so that the castle could not be supplied from the sea. In the end the king had to negotiate and Crichton only agreed to give up Blackness when he received the lands of Strathurd in exchange.

Even once Blackness was in royal hands, the fear remained that this stronghold might yet again be seized by the king's enemies and so during the childhood of James III to prevent any possibility of this it was decided that the castle should be demolished.

This delighted the merchants of Blackness — they had long been protesting about being forced to pay a kind of medieval danger money for the protection of their ships by the castle and they were now given permission to recover some of this expense by utilising the stones from its battlements to build a new pier.

Fortunately for the castle, however, the merchants were slow to act and in 1476 the right was withdrawn.

Just how important Blackness was can be judged from the amount of manoeuvring for its possession during the troubled reign of Mary, Queen of Scots. During her childhood in France the castle was garrisoned by French troops, who held it despite two attacks by Mary's enemies.

On another occasion it was the French soldiers themselves who went on the attack when they sailed across the Forth and "spoulzeit several of the Fife touns," before returning to Blackness with considerable booty.

Later in Mary's reign, in 1573, Sir James Kirkcaldy brought from France one year's income from her French dowry to help her cause in Scotland. He could not deliver the money to Edinburgh Castle, as it was besieged by the followers of the young James VI, so he decided to take it to Blackness where he believed the governor to be on the Queen's side.

Unfortunately, the governor saw the money as his chance to buy his pardon from the Regent Morton. Without hesitation he changed sides and had Kirkcaldy clapped in irons. While the governor rode off with his prize, Kirkcaldy persuaded the soldiers to revert to support of the Queen and to set him free, imprisoning, instead, the governor's brother, who had been left in charge.

It was then that the Regent Morton decided to use Kirkcaldy's wife to recapture the castle. Word was sent to Lady Kirkcaldy to tell her of her husband's safe return from France and, of course, she summoned her servants and rode the twenty miles to Blackness. That night the taper lights in the half-shuttered windows of the stern tower burnt late as Sir James entertained his wife, but, at length, Lady Kirkcaldy insisted that she must ride for home. It needed little persuasion to convince Sir James that he accompany her on the first part of the journey and that he should take most of the castle garrison as an escort.

They did not ride far, however, for, on the rise above the village, Captain Andrew Lambie and his men waited in ambush and, as Kirkcaldy and his men crested the rise, they they were seized. To his fury, Sir James saw his wife ride free. Sir James was imprisoned in Edinburgh, but eight days later he escaped. Shortly afterwards Lady Kirkcaldy was found strangled, murdered in her own bedroom, a deed for which Sir James paid the capital penalty.

Incidents such as this abound in the history of Blackness because, for more than two hundred years, the castle was used as one of Scotland's state prisons. Many of its captives were religious prisoners, ranging from Cardinal Beaton to John Knox's son-in-law, the Rev. John Welsh.

Welsh was one of six leading Scottish clergy imprisoned by James VI for daring to claim that they had the right to meet in General Assembly without him. Even after months shut up in Blackness they refused to acknowledge the king's prerogative and their defiance enjoyed great popular support, while Lady Culross assured them that "the darkness of Blackness was not the blackness of darkness".

Shortly afterwards, a prisoner of a very different shade of religious belief, Gilbert Brown, Abbot of New Abbey, was lodged in the Main Mast Tower for being a "trafficing and seducing Papist". Then, in 1624, it was the turn of an Edinburgh bailie, William Rigg, to be imprisoned. He had dared to challenge the teachings of the Episcopal Church. His was not a lone voice, however, and soon a whole stream of Covenanting prisoners were to experience the horrors of the dungeons of Blackness, most graphically described by Adam Blackader, son of the great Covenanting leader, who wrote of a dungeon "full of puddocks and toads".

This may well have been the most dreadful of the cells at Blackness, the Black Pit, which was situated right in the bows of the castle jutting out into the Forth and into which the river water flooded at high tide, not to drown the prisoners, as some tales would have it, but to provide the only primitive means of sanitation.

Lord Ochiltree was left to rot for more than twenty years in the prison for having dared to accuse the Duke of Hamilton of treason. He might have been left even longer at Blackness had it not been for Oliver Cromwell's capture of the castle. During the Commonwealth period, while Cromwell's republicans held the castle, an explosion occurred at Blackness in 1652. According to local legend, as the flash lit up the battlements the Devil was plainly seen.

It was, in fact, as an explosives store that the castle ended its active career for while there is no truth in the popular belief that the Act of Union of 1707 guaranteed the garrisoning of Blackness, soldiers were based there until after the First World War.

Blackness was ideally suited for this purpose as the explosives could be brought in by sea and landed at the castle's own pier—thus avoiding the danger of an overland journey. These cargoes of explosives were the last to be imported through Blackness as its civilian trade had long since disappeared with the growth of the better dock facilities three miles up river at Bo'ness, and the refusal of the Government to grant the village a licence to trade in tobacco, which had been its main export to Holland.

This decision resulted in the departure of the Mitchell family who re-established themselves in Glasgow, where they are to this day one of Britain's leading tobacco companies as well as one of the city's main benefactors, with gifts such as the famous Mitchell Library.

During Victorian times, attempts were made to turn Blackness into one of the new watering places which were all the rage, but although a few family holiday homes were built along the shore by families from Edinburgh and Falkirk little came of the idea and Blackness turned into the quiet backwater which it now is.

On one day each year, however, Blackness does regain some of the bustle which it knew as a thriving port with a prosperous trade with the Low Countries, for on the first Tuesday after the second Thursday in June, the Provost and Magistrates of Linlithgow come riding into the village on their annual inspection of the Marches.

Ceremonies at Blackness, which was given to Linlithgow by the royal charter of King Robert II in 1389 and where the Guilds of the royal burgh had their massive stone warehouse called the Guildry, begin with the laying of a wreath on the War Memorial at the entrance to the village outside the unusually designed little church, then all concerned pause for a moment to recover from the bumpy ride down from Low Port and enjoy a refreshing glass of Blackness Milk, which is somewhat more potent than the milk normally obtained from cows in these part on the other 364 days in the year, as it is liberally laced with whisky.

Thus revived all the participants then crowd into the small garden behind Flemings Tea Rooms in the Square, to hear the Baron Bailie's annual report.

Today the post of Baron Bailie is very much a sinecure and apart from this annual report he has few duties, but such was most certainly not the case in days gone by. For the Baron Bailie had to administer law and order in this far flung outpost of Linlithgow's empire. It was in fact because the Provost, Magistrates and Bailies of Linlithgow felt that Blackness was too cut off from the burgh that the Baron Bailies were originally appointed and they had full rights to administer fines and other punishments.

The right to appoint a separate Baron Bailie for Blackness dates right back to the original royal charter of King Robert II in 1389 and apart from a few years during the Commonwealth of Oliver Cromwell between 1649 and 1660 has existed as a right to the present day, when Baron Bailie Robert Fleming keeps the old tradition faithfully alive.

In the past when the Marches had a more practical purpose rather than the simple pleasures of today, the business of this court, which was variously referred to as the Head Court of Blackness or the Court of St. Ninian, whose chapel was in the village, included various items both civil and criminal such as trials for breach of the peace, actions for debt and even the admission in 1696 of the Governor of Blackness Castle and his steward as Burgesses and "Guid Brethern".

In 1658 the Marches were ridden on Saturday 8th June and it is minuted that at the court at Blackness, the pier, harbour and greens of Blackness, proving unprofitable it was resolved to offer them on lease to two local sea captains, Matthew Caldom and David Drysdale. It must have been a very eventful court for Caldom because the same day he was indicted for keeping "swine" that "howked in his neighbours' lands and in the greens". One other item of business from the same Marches day court was the creation of William Bell, Merchant of Blackness as a burgess and a "Guild Brother".

Now the court at Blackness has no formal matters to transact, but each year the tradition of having a separate Baron Bailie is still maintained and he is re-appointed at the court, which is held high on Castle Hill on the ancient site of St. Ninian's Chapel. There bowers are erected and these leafy arches are thought to be links with times older even than the chapel which was occupied the site, for it is suggested that they go right back to pagan times, when they indicated a wish for fertility for the lands on which they were erected and for the beasts which grazed on them. When Christain times arrived the bowers were preserved and adapted into part of the religious ceremony of the priest blessing the fields and so they remain until today.

Upon the arrival of the Provost, Magistrates and the Baron Bailie accompanied by the whole crowd of burgesses both from the village and Linlithgow the court on the hill begins with the reading of this proclamation, "I defend and I forbid in our Sovereign Lady's name and in the name of My Lord Povost and Bailies of the Royal Burgh of Linlithgow that no person or persons trouble or molest this court nor one speak for another without leave first asked and then given under all highest pains, that after may follow. God Save the Queen."

As soon as the proclamation is finished the Town Clerk proceeds to summon the vassals before the court. In the past the vassals included all the local landowners such as The Right Hon. John Adrian Louis of Hopetoun, Andrew Gilmour, Esq., farmer of Blackness, John Ritchie Esq., farmer of Blackness, Henry Cadell, Esq., of Grange and Alexander Aitken, Esq., of Falkirk.

After the vassals have paid due homage, the Baron Bailie is then appointed or re-appointed and the court is formally adjourned for "a twelve month, excepting riots".

Business complete the Provost and all of the others then make their way down from Castle Hill to lunch. The menu for one eighteenth century Marches lunch held in the inn in the Square at Blackness read,

"Two dish of ffryed chickens	£3	4	6
Ane dish of salmond	1	10	0
Ane pudding	2	0	0
For Rost mutton	3	10	0
Lamb	2	8	0
Gooseberries and sugar	1	1	0
Vinegar and sugar to the sellets		17	6
Bread	1	0	0
Ane choppin of brandy	2	0	0
To gardinars and he cook ane mutchkin of brandy	1	0	0
Nineteen bottles of wine	19	0	0
Ale	1	16	0

Today lunch is a cold buffet meal served in a marquee on the lawn below the castle battlements and following the meal speeches and fraternising fill the afternoon.

On Marches Day 1911 the toast list at Blackness read,
"The King,
"Queen Mary and other members of the Royal Family
"The Provosts and Visitors from other Burghs
"The Convention of Royal Burghs
"The Clergy
"The Town Council of Linlithgow,
and the official programme stressed that speeches must be limited to five minutes each.

After the speeches a delegation is sent to present My Lord Provosts compliments to the Dyers who also lunch in the village and representatives of the Dyers return the compliment.

On the way up the steep hill out of Blackness it's worth stopping to look at the unusual little village church with its central steeple, which was built specially during the First World War to provide a place of worship for the ships' companies of the many naval vessels which anchored off the village out in the Forth.

For real church history, however, it is necessary to move on to the next parish down river, because there Abercorn Church can not only claim to be of Norman origin, but can also claim to have been mentioned several times in the works of the early church historian, the Venerable Bede.

Abercorn Church

As West Lothian's smallest school, the twenty-pupil Abercorn Primary, completes a year of centenary celebrations, it's interesting to look at its first and most famous dominie, Christopher Dawson.

For Dawson was a dominie whose methods were a century before their time and it was because of his progressive ideas that he was invited to move from his first school in Cupar to become master of the old church school at Abercorn, which served the children of the Marquess of Linlithgow's Hopetoun Estate near South Queensferry.

The beautiful, spacious Hopetoun Estate overlooking the Forth was in marked contrast to the cramped and crowded little school which Dawson found waiting for him and so, without delay, he set about turning the grounds of the big house, with its deer park and the shores of the river, into his open-air classroom.

Hopetoun's estate workers, foresters and farm labourers stopped and stared in amazement as the new dominie led his brood Pied Piper-like on nature rambles, which lend a familiar ring to Lothian Education Authority's newly published 1978 Environmental Studies report urging teachers to get their pupils out on field studies.

Back in the classroom, despite the huddle of benches and desks, Dawson found room for his pupils to set up their own school museum. Most of the items the boys and girls gathered for themselves, displays on local geology and botany taking pride of place, but more exotic additions were provided by the many visitors to Hopetoun House, who often brought gifts from their foreign travels.

After school, too, dominie Dawson organised extra curricular activities, taking his pupils swimming and on fishing expeditions. Dawson's informal approach did not, however, mean that his young scholars lacked discipline, for they knew full well that "the maister" could wield the tawse as capably as the fishing rod.

"Be careful to check the smallest acts of disobedience and you will never be troubled with any great ones," he wrote, but while he was quite prepared to make his presence felt and strap his new scholars into shape, he eventually had his own unique method of abolishing corporal punishment as, is described by his niece Jean Butler.

For in her biography of her uncle she wrote: "One day in school an interesting and amusing ceremony took place. The faithful tawse which had proved such a useful ally during the first few months were declared to have served their purpose and outlived their usefulness and were solemnly cut in pieces, some of the girls carrying away the bits as trophies of a bygone age."

Any doubt, which parents might have had about their dominie's unusual approach to both lessons and discipline, so very different from the strict formal traditional methods of neighbouring masters in Bo'ness and Linlithgow, were dispelled at the annual inspections when the parish minister and the whole of his kirk session turned up to examine the bairns and expressed themselves entirely satisfied with the results, despite the until then unheard of means used to obtain them.

In 1874, however, Dawson's freedom to teach in his own way was suddenly threatened when the government decided to regularise Scotland's schools and inflexible dictates about curriculum and methods were issued in far off London.

Many of the old style dominies decided to resign and accept the pensions which they were offered rather than try to adapt the new regime complete with its fear inspiring inspectors, but Dawson despite complaining that: "It is now expected that children shall be regularly turned out by the gross like so many little human vessels duly warranted to contain a certain amount of knowledge," stuck to his post.

Despite complaining that he had been reduced to "nothing more than a grant earning machine," Dawson still managed to bring his own flair to the methods insisted on by the new Department of Education and opened an hour early each morning to gain time for his own ideas, without endangering his pupils' chances in the official tests.

Dawson's determination paid off, because in the first official inspection he was granted "the highest possible grant for discipline and organisation". He was also rewarded by the building of the fine new grey stone gothic school building at White Quarries, which last month celebrated one hundred years of education within its walls.

Soon after it was completed in the autumn of 1878 dominie Dawson found himself with more pupils than ever before, because the opening of a shale mine in the district brought a sudden influx of miners' families.

These rough, tough youngsters were a new challenge for the now aging schoolmaster, but he met it just as he did many others including the education of a young Turkish boy who was a guest at Hopetoun.

Dawson taught on in the new school for twenty-one years, until on September 11, he laid down his chalk and his pointer for the last time and retired after completing exactly fifty years of teaching, no fewer than forty-three of them in the same parish of Abercorn.

Today, Abercorn Primary School's roll has shrunk drastically since the days a century ago when the miners' children stretched its accommodation to the limit, but under its present head teacher, Mrs Jean Patterson, it has retained the progressive pioneering spirit which its first dominie gave it, with educational outings to places as far away as Orkney.

Now, instead of shale oil, it is North Sea oil which recently brought a stir to the playground at Abercorn, for the vast pipeline taking the oil to Hound Point for export runs right by it.

So, too, does the M9 motorway and it was from it that a film director spotted the little old school with the result that the Abercorn youngsters will finish their one hundredth anniversary festivities with the novel experience of seeing themselves on television advertising a well-known soup.

Somehow I think Christopher Dawson would have been delighted as he would no doubt also be with the fact the nature trails which he pioneered through the Hopetoun woods are now available to all schools which care to visit the education centre set up recently.

"Old Dawson isn't a bad sort, if only you do what he tells you," wrote one of his pupils. Now one hundred years later, perhaps the dominie of Abercorn's methods still has something to tell the teachers of today.

Abercorn's main claim to fame nowadays, is of being the site of what must surely rank as being the stateliest of Scotland's stately homes, the magnificent Adam Mansion, Hopetoun House, Home of the Marquess of Linlithgow.

Hopetoun House is undoubtedly the most magnificent of all of West Lothian's famous homes and indeed it must rate as one of the most magnificent homes in the whole country.

Occupying a superb setting overlooking the two Forth Bridges it was built by the first Earl of Hopetoun and is recognised as Scotland's finest Adam mansion. The interior is equally impressive with apartments created and adorned by Adam's sons Robert and John and furnished by Chippendale's rival James Cullen, who designed many pieces especially for the great house.

Recently Hopetoun has been restored to their original style and usage, including the famous parade rooms through which King George IV promenaded during his famous Scottish visit.

Among Hopetoun's attractions for visitors is a well laid out museum, which depicts the Hope family's considerable contribution to British diplomacy, including former Marquis of Linlithgows careers as Viceroys in Australia and India. Probably the most popular exhibit with the many children who visit the house each year in school parties, is a stuffed Emu, brought home live from Australia and which roamed the grounds for many years.

Today the estate does not boast anything quite as exotic as an Emu, but it does possess peacocks, tumbler pigeons and other ornamental birds as well as the herds of fallow and red deer and a flock of St. Kilda sheep with their magnificent horns, all of which can be seen on a well laid out nature trail.

No look at the Hopetoun animals can however be complete without visiting the stables, where even the horses knew their place with separate sections for hunters, carriage horses and work horses. Now a special exhibition about horses in Scotland occupies the stable block, which was carefully designed with imitation windows in order to maintain the symmetry of the architecture, which makes Hopetoun such a delight to look at and which well justifies its claim to be Scotland's Versailles.

A short detour inland leads up the hill from Hopetoun to Woodend. It is worth keeping to the high ground and the modern main road for another few hundred yards to admire the sweeping panoramic views of the Forth from the village of Newton, whose colourful flower beds make it one of the most attractive wee places in West Lothian.

There, former county councillor Bob Lowden claims to run Scotland's oldest filling station, established as long ago as 1889 by his wife's family, the Greenfields.

It was in that year that Mrs Lowden's grandfather surprised the neighbours when he became one of West Lothian's first car owners. Young Mr Greenfield bought a Benz, but discovered that there was no motor spirit in Scotland, as fuel was called in those days long before the term petrol had been thought of.

To obtain the vital motor spirit Mr Greenfield had to send all the way to London to the sole suppliers, Carless, Cappell and Leonard, who sent it north by sea to Leith, from whence he had to fetch the two-gallon cans by horse-drawn cart.

Rather than go to all this trouble just to supply himself, Mr Greenfield added the cans of motor fuel to the range of goods which he already sold in the village store at Newton, and soon found himself with customers, including the Marquess from nearby Hopetoun House and others who motored all the way from Glasgow to obtain supplies.

The two-gallon cans were sold for 10½d and that included a forty per cent profit," laughed Mr Lowden as he filled up my car at his modern pumps, which lave long since replaced the first hand pump installed in 1908.

From Newton village it is possible to drive straight on along the main road into Queensferry, passing Dundas Castle on the right hand side on the way, but at this point there is one of the few stretches of coast road along this part of the river, and it would be a pity not to use it.

It leads through the pleasant little hamlet of Society on to Port Edgar Naval Base. Port Edgar is said to take its name from Prince Edgar, the brother of Queen Margaret after whom the ferry is named.

Chapter 10

The Queensferry Passage

According to tradition, Margaret and her brother were fleeing from the English court following the Norman Conquest, when their ship was blown off course and sought shelter in the Forth. They landed at what is now called Port Edgar, and discovered that the Scottish court was then at Dunfermline.

And so the royal voyagers duly sailed on across the Forth to the wooded headland, still named after Princess Margaret, and on to the royal court. There she became Queen on her marriage to King Malcolm Canmore and started the ferry to take them both safely to and from the castle at Edinburgh. Thus the names North Queensferry and the royal burgh of Queensferry (never South unless you want to raise the ire of its inhabitants) were added to the map.

As well as providing safe passage for herself and the King, Margaret was also anxious to encourage pilgrims to visit the shrine at St Andrews and so she insisted that the crossing chould be free for those Christians on their way to worship.

The Queen's Ferry must indeed have been a most religious place for Margaret gave the charter to operate it to the monks of Dunfermline Abbey and, for many years, it appears to have been the priests themselves who rowed travellers across what could often be a very rough stretch of water.

One monarch who found it thus was Queen Margaret's own son who became Alexander I. In 1123 he was caught in the Forth by a severe gale and was driven ashore on the island of Inchcolm. There he found shelter in a hermit's tiny cell, which to this day is thought to survive just to the west of the still magnificent Augustinian abbey, which King Alexander founded to show his thanks for his rescue from the cruel waters.

Less fortunate was Alexander III, who reached Queensferry late one

Highway in the sky. Walkers crowded the new Forth Road Bridge on its opening day, Friday 4th September, 1964.

dark and stormy night. Despite the pleas of the ferrymen to rest for the night and wait to cross at dawn. Alexander, eager to get home to his wife in Kinghorn, demanded to be rowed across. Despite the battering of the waves they made the other side, but as the King rode on along the Fife shore in the dark and wind, his horse stumbled and he plunged over the cliff to his death at Pettycur, about a mile from Kinghorn, thus pitching Scotland into more years of strife.

By the reign of James VI and I, more peaceful times had come to Scotland, but the weather still caused him trouble at Queensferry, when in 1617 he made his first royal tour of Scotland since his accession to the English throne fourteen years earlier.

The river was rough and unwelcoming when the royal party reached North Queensferry, but anxious to reach the comparative civilisation of Holyrood before nightfall the King embarked.

He reached the southern shore in safety, but one of the accompanying fleet of small boats was less fortunate and several of his followers were drowned. For years after the accident, it was rumoured that a large quantity of the royal silver table ware also went to the bottom, thus giving us a Scottish version of how King John lost his treasure in the Wash.

After the Reformation, the rights of the ferry were divided into sixteen parts, the owners of which were each entitled to operate one vessel on the passage.

By the beginning of the seventeenth century, the Queen's ferry was one of the busiest in Scotland, but in 1602 all sailings were banned in an effort to prevent the plague, which was then rampant in Edinburgh from spreading to Fife and the north.

However, the plague soon died down and the ferry became busy again. Just how important it was considered is clearly shown by the fact that during the 1700s the very first turnpike road in Scotland was constructed to link it with Edinburgh.

Traffic using the turnpike had to pay tolls, so the idea of charging for use of the Forth Road Bridge is clearly no new one. When it was opened the turnpike, which ran past New Halls and Muttonhole at the Hawes Inn and Davidson's Mains were then known, was considered the finest of its kind in Britain. But travellers were less happy about the state of the actual ferry.

Their complaints increased steadily after 1784 when the ferry rights were put up for annual public auction, the operators being more concerned about recouping their outlay and making a profit than about the service they offered.

Passengers complained that the piers, especially on the South Queensferry side of the Forth were in a ruinous condition; that there was no superintendent in charge of the boats; that the ferrymen were sometimes not very sober; and most annoying of all, there were frequent occasions when there were no boats available at South Queensferry as all the ferrymen had their homes at North Queensferry.

In the end an act of Parliament was passed in 1809 appointing trustees to look after the ferry and from then on it was managed in a most business like fashion.

Not just one, but two superintendents were appointed, and it was laid down that the boatmen must never be called up to serve in the Navy. The act also stated that no more than two-thirds of the boats must be at the same side at any time and a scale of charges was drawn up.

For the hire of a small boat by day the charge was 2s 6d, but if a traveller arrived after dark then the cost doubled to 5s. Both by day and night, however, certain people escaped paying completely. They included express horsemen from the post office, soldiers, volunteers, provided they were in uniform, and vagrants, who had legal passes.

The biggest change of all to affect the ferry came in 1821 with the introduction for the first time of a steamship, which was appropriately called the Queen Margaret.

The Queen Margaret, which cost all of £2369 to build and £12 14s a week including the crew's wages, to operate, was very much the wonder of the age, for not only did whe cut the passage time to a mere twenty minutes, but if the wind fell, she could always tow the other sailing boats.

The new regulations and the new steam ferry combined to make the Queensferry passage one of the safest in the country, but a serious accident did occur at the very beginning of Queen Victoria's reign.

The accident happened not during a crossing of the river but on the pier opposite to the Hawes Inn, when in October 1838 a coach crashed off it into the water.

Despite the frantic efforts of the boatmen, the young woman and her female servant, who were its sole occupants were both drowned, before they were pulled free.

A much happier event took place at the ferry four years after this tragedy when the young Queen Victoria, accompanied by Prince Albert, made the crossing on September 5, 1842.

By this time, traffic had increased to such an extent that the little Queen Margaret had been replaced by what a contemporary account describes as a "very superior seaboat, the William Adam, length ninety-eight feet and breadth thirty-two, which leaves the south side every hour and the north side every half hour, from sunrise to sunset".

The same account goes on to describe the Queen's crossing as follows: "The William Adam was honoured by conveying Queen Victoria across the firth on her royal progress to the north".

"The day was most beautiful; the water unruffled; the crowds on both shores very great; the sea covered by numerous steamers and boats, gaily adorned; indeed the whole scene was calculated to make an impression not speedily to be forgotten".

"It is understood that the Sovereign expressed the greatest satisfaction with all the arrangements made on board the steamer. Mr Mason, the superintendent, took the helm, while the attentive skipper, Charles Roxburgh, attended to the other duties."

By a strange coincidence, over a century later, it was another Mr Mason, Mr R. A. Mason, who as ferry superintendent made all the arrangements and accompanied our present Queen, when, after opening and making the first official crossing of the new Road Bridge on September 4, 1964, Her Majesty sailed back to the old Hawes Pier at South Queensferry on the last crossing made by the modern electric paddle ferry, Queen Margaret.

And so the ferry started by a queen crossing the Forth ended with a queen making the same passage.

Now the smart white and black painted Queen Margaret, Robert the Bruce, Mary Queen of Scots, and Sir William Wallace, and all the other ferries which before them regularly plied to and fro to maintain the Queen's ferry are only memories.

When it first opened the Road Bridge was the largest suspension bridge in Europe and the fourth largest in the world. It now ranks second in Europe to Portugal's Salazar Bridge across the Tagus at Lisbon.

The centre span of the Forth Road Bridge is 3,300 feet long with two side spans each 1340 feet long, a southern approach viaduct of 1437 feet and a northern viaduct of 842 feet making a total length of a little over one-and-a-half miles.

The deck is suspended by steel wire rope hangers from two main cables which stretch in one length of 7,000 feet from anchorage to anchorage and pass over the tops of the main towers. These towers are 512 feet high, made up of welded steel units fastened together with large high-strength alloy steel bolts. The cables consist of some 12,000 galvanized high tensile steel wires, one fifth of an inch in diameter which are hung in position one at a time, bundled into strands, secured at the anchorages and finally compacted into a circular shape 2 feet in diameter.

The deck provides two roadways 24 feet wide, two cycle tracks 9 feet wide and two footpaths 6 feet wide, and its lowest point is 150 feet above river level.

The approximate quantities of steel used in various parts of the bridge were

Towers	6,000 Tons
Cables	8,000 Tons
Suspended deck	16,000 Tons
Reinforcement in concrete	6,000 Tons
Various	3,000 Tons
	39,000 Tons

The new Road Bridge completed in 1964 was not the first planned to span the Forth at this point. As early as 1818 James Anderson, an Edinburgh engineer, produced detailed plans for a chain suspension road bridge. His bridge was to have a 25 foot wide carriageway with footpaths on either side. The main spans were to have been 1500 feet long and were to have been made of Swedish steel treated with linseed oil, which he maintained would prevent rust and therefore do away with the need for painting

American oak was to be used for the roadway which was to be surfaced with a mixture of gravel, sand and chalk bound together with pitch and tar. While Anderson had done his homework well, he had chosen a bad time to put forward his proposals which he costed at £175,000. They were rejected as much too costly for the country to bear as "it was still impoverished following the long war against Napoleon".

A road bridge was not the only alternative proposed for the Queensferry during the nineteenth century. Several Victorian engineers saw a tunnel as the solution.

Thousands of tourists will travel out to South Queensferry this summer to admire the slender elegance of the new Road Bridge and the massive magnificence of the old Forth Bridge. When the railway line to the North was first carried across the river at Queensferry in 1890 however, the huge cantilever Forth Bridge was not admired by everyone and some surprisingly harsh comments were written about its appearance.

One of its fiercest critics was the travel writer Stewart Dick, who, in his book, "The Pageant of the Forth", wrote. "It is a strange thing that so wonderful a monument of engineering skill as the Forth Bridge

The building of the new Forth Bridge

should be so unsightly. Certainly had the building been of wood or stone and rightly constructed no matter how plain the design, the result would have been pleasing to the eye."

Mr Dick went on to mourn the fact that in the past the old builders had felt that any of their important works should be enriched by all means in their power; by arches, parapets and towers, all executed lovingly to please the eye, whereas the builders of the Forth Bridge had obviously not cared how their finished work looked. "Callous indifference", complained Mr Dick had been shown "to all aesthetic feeling".

The feature of the bridge which most infuriated Mr Dick was its famous triple spans which he would have liked to have seen carried on skyward to end in soaring spires, instead of being "cut off bluntly on top the moment their utilitarian purpose is achieved".

The Forth Bridge's almost legendery paintwork was, as far as Mr Dick was concerned, the ultimate insult. Instead of the, "cheapest possible coat of red lead," he declared that he would have given the bridge a new glory by the use of gold paint.

Mr Dick's golden Forth Bridge has never come to pass, but a short distance up river we now have our new silver roadway in the sky. At the end of his criticism of the railway bridge Mr Dick stated, "Perhaps in the future some modern engineer, who is also an artist, will design a bridge that is beautiful as well as strong; but not until he gives us something more than we have in the Forth Bridge". Now we have that second Forth Bridge, but we will never know if Mr Dick would have admired its sleek streamlined beauty as much as the thousands of visitors to Queensferry undoubtably do.

The recent death of the designer of the Forth Road Bridge, Sir Gilbert Robert makes this an opportune time to consider a memorial to this great architect, whose work also included the Severn Suspension Bridge.

What better form could this memorial take than a visitor display centre on the lines of the National Trust's much admired Bannockburn audio visual show, telling the story in pictures and sounds of the building of Queensferry's two great showpieces.

And the display would include the history of the ferry which plied for eight hundred years before the completion of the first Forth Bridge in 1891 and of its graceful companion Road Bridge in September 1964.

The ideal setting for the bridge Centre is Queensferry's ancient and now disused Parish Church, situated midway between the massive Victorian cantilever railway bridge and the slender, modern suspension road bridge. In its graveyard are buried some of the local men who gave their lives building the earlier bridge.

Imagine the centre to have a giant floor-to-the-ceiling map of the river showing clearly why Queensferry is the natural spot to cross the Forth as travellers have always done right down through the centuries.

A mock-up of the scene at the Hawes Pier could be devised with a sou'wester-clad ferryman waiting to take tickets for the crossing — in a rowing boat.

The boat, built on the lines of the old, fairground rib-tickler, could heave realistically as the passengers watch and listen to the story of the shipwreck of Princess Margaret her subsequent marriage to the Scottish king Malcolm Canmore and her setting up of the ferry.

Highlights of the story would then be told with slides of the Fife shore, sound effects of thunder, a flash of lightning and a simulated storm of the kind which must have raged on the night King Alexander made his fatal crossing eager to reach his young French wife. He died when his horse stumbled and plunged over the cliffs near Kinghorn.

At the end, visitors will appreciate why travellers were so relieved when the Forth rail bridge was completed and became one of the modern wonders of the Victorian age.

Giant blow-up photographs of the bridge in the course of construction and mementos of the official opening by the Prince of Wales could lead visitors to seats in a Victorian railway carriage. Through the windows visualise film of the girders rushing by interspersed with slide shots of the magnificent views of the Forth, up and down river.

To round off this section — scenes from John Buchan's "The 39 Steps" showing Kenneth More in his famous role as Sir Richard Hannay escaping from the train and diving from the bridge.

Next, a section about other famous bridge stories, such as the true one about Tommy Burn's night plunge from the bridge in the 1890s and German attacks on the bridge as a vital communications link during the Second World War.

The end of the war brought with it the big build-up in motor traffic,which finally led to the building of the Road Bridge. A ten-minute multi-media presentation of its construction from the spinning of the first steel strands to its completion and official opening on the misty morning of Friday, September 4, 1964, by Queen Elizabeth would complete the story.

At present visitors can only stand and stare from the bridge car park,

As workers spun the web of the new suspension bridge. Photographer John Doherty caught the old ferry and the Victorian Railway Bridge in the background.

buy a postcard and drive away again. The Bridge Centre would bring visitors down into the centre of Queensferry to the obvious benefit of the Royal and Ancient Burgh's shops and cafes.

One thing which summer visitors to Edinburgh will not be able to do is enjoy a pleasure cruise on the Forth. For despite the efforts of MP Mr Tam Dalyell, who raised the matter in Parliament, there are still no sailings down the river.

Today's lack of pleasure sailings on the Forth is rather ironical, because with the coming of steam power, it was one of the first rivers in the world where passenger steamers were introduced.

Pleasure sailings on the Forth in fact began with the very first practical steam ship of all, Henry Bell's "Comet," which was sent for her first annual overhaul to the shipbuilding yard of Shawland & Hart at Bo'ness.

By the time that the overhaul was completed, curiosity about the little "Comet" had increased to such an extent that all the local gentlemen, who could afford it, agreed to pay the sum of 7s 6d each to sail aboard her down river to Leith.

So great was the interest aroused in the Forth ports by the "Comets" visit in 1813, that later the same year, several local businessmen backed a Mr Bell (not the steamship inventor) to buy the steamer "Stirling," which had just been launched at Greenock, to operate her on the river.

The venture seems to have proved successful because in 1815 the "Stirling" was joined by the first two steamers built on the Forth, the "Lady of the Lake" and the "Morning Star," both of which were built in Kincardine, where they were launched on the same day.

Mr Bell had however been over ambitious as there was not enough business for all three steamers and so reluctantly he was forced to sell his new "Lady of the Lake," to German owners.

Two years later, he was convinced that the number of passengers had increased sufficiently to make three boats pay, and so he bought back the "Lady," which soon began the long voyage home from Hamburg.

Finding sufficient passengers was not the only difficulty which the River Forth's first steamship owner had to face. He had also to overcome the problem of literally getting them on board his ships, for the steamers had arrived so suddenly that to begin with there were no sutiable piers for them at many of the Forth ports.

At Newhaven, for instance, until 1818 intending passengers had either to be rowed out to the steamers or had to take the chance of getting their feet soaked on a primitive gangway mounted on wheels, which was rolled out into the river, when one of the steamers arrived.

Despite these early difficulties Mr Bell survived until 1826, when he heard that several Stirling business men were putting up £4500 to found the Stirling, Alloa & Kincardine Steamboat Company.

As a shrewd business man Mr Bell realised that there were not enough passengers on the Forth for two companies and so he approached the Stirling men and offered to save them the time and trouble of building steamers for themselves, by selling them his three for exactly £4500.

And so the "Stirling," the "Lady of the Lake" and the "Morning Star" changed hands, and the monopoly on the Forth continued for almost ten more years.

In 1835, however, the Stirling, Alloa & Kincardine Company was challenged by a Mr Barclay from Glasgow, who brought the "Benalmond" from the Clyde. This time neither side would give way and so a series of steamer battles soon developed with the boats of the rival owners racing to be first in at the piers.

Just how crazy, yet how satisfyingly exciting these river tussles were, was recorded by an American travel writer, Mr N. P. Willis, who unwittingly found himself involved in one, when he decided to travel by steamer from Stirling to Granton.

"At Stirling," he later wrote, "I had a running fight for my portmanteau and carpet bag, from the hotel to the pier, and was at last embarked in the entirely wrong boat, by sheer force of pulling and lying. The two steamers, the "Victoria" and the "Benalmond," got under way together; the former, in which I was a compulsory passenger, having a flageolet and a bass drum by way of a band, and the other a dozen lusty performers and most of the company.

"The river was very narrow and the tide down and although the other seemed the better boat, we had the bolder pilot and were lighter laden and twice as desperate.

"Whenever we were quite abreast and the wheels touched with the narrowness of the river, we marched our flageolet and bass drum close to the enemy and gave them a blast, 'to waken the dead,' taking occasion, during our moments of defeat, to recover and ply the principal musician with beer and encouragement.

"The two pilots stood broad on, their legs, every muscle on the alert, and although the "Benalmond" wore the cleaner jacket, "Victoria" had the "varminter" look. He was the wickedest of all wicked things, a wicked Scotchman—a sort of saint turned sinner.

"As we approached a sharp bend in the course of the stream, I perceived by the countenance of our pilot, that it was to be the critical moment.

The "Benalmond" was a little ahead but we had the advantage of the inside of the course and very soon with the commencement of the curve we gained sensibly on the enemy and I saw clearly that we would cut her off by a half-boat's length.

The flageolet made all split again with, "The Campbells are Comin'," the bass drum was never so belaboured and, "Up with your helm," cried every voice as we came at the rate of twelve miles in the hour, sharp on to the angle of mud and bullrushes and to our utter surprise the pilot jammed down her tiller and ran the battered nose of the "Victoria" plumb in upon the enemy's forward quarter.

"The next moment we were going it like man down the middle of the river and far astern stuck the "Benalmond" in the mud, her paddles driving her deeper at every stroke, her music hushed and the crowd on her deck standing speechless with amazement. The flageolet and bass drum marched aft and played louder than ever and we were soon in the open Firth and without competition to the sleeping isle of Inchkeith.

For one period of each summer there was no need for the rival companies to do battle with each other for passengers. This was when the Navy put into the Forth and crowds of people from Edinburgh and the other towns along the shores of the river queued for trips on the paddlers so that they could catch a closer glimpse of the great "wooden walls".

Sometimes the public were allowed aboard the great wooden hulled battleships and this made the steamers even busier as they ferried the crowds out from Queensferry.

As the years passed the "wooden walls" were replaced by dreadnoughts, but still a sail on the river to see the fleet remained a summer must.

An advertisement in the Bo'ness "Journal" in 1914 invited the local people to take advantage of special evening cruises by Wilson's commodious steamers at a charge on only 6d each.

Within months, several of the Forth steamers themselves became part

of that fleet when they were commandeered by the Admiralty.
After the First World War, pleasure sailings were resumed on the Forth and one of the most popular vessels was the Fair Maid, a model of which was recently presented to Grangemouth Burgh museum.

Built by McKnight's of Ayr in 1866 and launched as the "Madge Wildfire," she was already over forty years old when she began her new life on the Forth after being bought by the Forth Towing Company of Grangemouth.

For most of the period from 1927 to 1939 the Fair Maid was based at the West Pier, Leith from where she sailed across the Firth to Aberdour and Kirkcaldy and up river to Kincardine and Alloa.

But on summer Saturdays she was often chartered for Sunday School outings from Bo'ness and Grangemouth and many of the older inhabitants of both towns still recall happily their trips as children aboard her to Burntisland.

With the outbreak of war in 1939 the "Fair Maid" was taken over by the Admiralty, as she had also been during the First World War, and by the time peace returned she was unfortunately fit only to go to the shipbreakers at Troon.

The "Fair Maid," was never replaced and apart from an ex-naval vessel, the TS MV Royal Lady, which operated in 1947 and the little MV Second Snark, operated by Denny Brothers of Dumbarton which provided short sightseeing cruises for tourists wanting to see the building of the Forth Road Bridge, there have been no pleasure sailings on the river since 1945.

November 28 was often a worrying day for many people in Scotland in years gone by. For the date was always "term time," when all rents had to be paid.

One group of people were however always confident that they would be able to pay up at "term time". They were the fishermen of the River Forth and they had a saying: "Never mind, they'll be up to pay the rent".

The "they" in the saying were the millions of small, silver sprats, shoals of which still arrive regularly in the Forth at this time of year.

Today the tiny sprats, which are little cousins of the herring, are usually thought fit only for fish meal, but in the eighteenth and nineteenth centuries there was a big demand for these little fish for smoking. Millions were crammed into barrels and exported to Germany and the Scandinavian countries and the profits provided a rich sea harvest for the Forth fishing families.

Not everyone, however, welcomed the coming each November of the sprats. For the catches as well as providing money to pay the rent also provided plenty of extra "siller" and according to reports at the time much of this was spent on drink.

One of the busiest centres of the November sprat fishing season was the little royal burgh of Queensferry and its parish minister, the Rev. Thomas Dimma, was gravely concerned not only about the marked increase in drunkenness which he blamed on the coming of the sprats, but also about the effect the fishing boom had on the morals of the little Forth port.

Mr Dimma explained his worries when he wrote in the Second Statistical Account of Scotland that: "Though this fish trade is most beneficial to the country at large, it is not favourable to the morality of the town. Forty or fifty carters are frequently in attendance and the consumption of ardent spirits is greatly increased. The carters, who are not generally of the most exemplary character cast an influence around the fishing season, which is most injurious to sound morals".

As well as the carters, the minister's moral worries were added to by the arrival of large numbers of fishermen who hurried from other ports to Queensferry to seize their share of the shoals of silver sprats.

From Fisharrow, Cellardyke, Prestonpans and Buckhaven, Mr Dimma estimated that as many as up to one hundred fishing boats jostled for position in Queensferry's congested little harbour.

To try to ease the chaos on the narrow stone quays the tax on each barrel of sprats, or Garvies as the "Ferry" folk often called them, was lowered from 4d if cured on the harbour side to only 2d if they were carted up into the town itself for gutting and salting.

No matter where the sprats were processed, however, as soon as the day's fishing was over and the catch safely ashore the crews of all the fishing boats joined the carters to crowd into Queensferry's "one inn, eight alehouses and four shops with accommodation provided for drinking," which, according to the minister, were "all most prejudicial to the morals of people".

Mr Dimma then went on to maintain that: "Accidents of a most frightful character have occurred almost every year from the immoderate use of spirits and though there have been deaths both by fire and water, the votaries of dissipation are neither improved nor diminished in number".

Queensferry's problems with its annual fishing invasion were in the end solved by the little silver sprats themselves because for some unexplained reason by the end of the nineteenth century they no longer seemed to favour the waters between the town and Queen Margaret's Hope on the Fife shore.

During the past few years small shoals of sprats have turned up and for a few brief days each November Queensferry enjoys a return of the bustle of its Victorian sprat fishing days.

Tastes have changed and as now few people apart from the Scandinavians and Germans enjoy eating them, most go for pet food or fish meal manufacture.

There is therefore no delay over curing and no excuse for the lorry drivers to dally in the "Queensferry Arms," the "Stag's Head" or any of the other pubs and bars overlooking the harbour, where the presence of their carter predecessors so worried the ministers and delighted the local lassies.

Chapter 11

Dalmeny House and Village

Scotland's "Mentmore" is the description which has inevitably been applied to Dalmeny House, near Queensferry, since Lord Rosebery's announcement this his Scottish seat is from 1981 to join the ranks of stately homes whose doors are flung open to the public.

For although Lord Rosebery sold many of the treasures of Mentmore in Buckinghamshire for more than £6 million in 1977 he first removed many of its finest pieces to Dalmeny where they now grace its high-ceilinged rooms with their magnificent views out across the River Forth to the hills of Fife.

Dalmeny estate, which stretches from Cramond to the Hawes Pier at Queensferry, was acquired by the Roseberys in 1662 and the handsome grey stone mansion was built for the fourth earl in 1814.

It was the first gothic revival house in Scotland designed by William Wilkins and it took three years to complete. Dating from the Napoleonic period, the house possesses an interesting collection of relics of the famous French leader. Outside the house fine golf links stretch down to the shores of the river.

Dalmeny House reached the height of its fame after the fourth earl was succeeded by his grandson, Archibald Philip Primrose, in 1868, for the new Lord Rosebery married one of the world's richest heiress, Hannah, daughter of Baron Meyer de Rothschild, and gained further nationwide publicity as one of the nineteenth century's most prominent Liberal politicians.

Despite being excluded from the House of Commons because of his earldom, his reputation as a social reformer and great public speaker grew steadily and in 1880 the Liberal party leader Gladstone came to stay at Dalmeny.

For weeks Dalmeny was never out of the headlines, because it was from there that Rosebery masterminded Gladstone's famous Midlothian Campaign, which completely revolutionised electioneering techniques. It brought the party leader to the people, who had recently been given the vote for the first time.

Gladstone was not the only distinguished visitor to Dalmeny House. Queen Victoria herself called in during one of her journeys to Balmoral and when in March 1894 Gladstone resigned as Prime Minister it was to Rosebery that the Queen turned to become the new Premier.

For the next ten years Rosebery battled with the major political controversies of the age, including home rule for Ireland about which he quarrelled violently with his Liberal colleague Campbell-Bannerman. Thus, when the rival Conservative government fell in December 1905 and Bannerman was asked by the King to form a cabinet. Rosebery retired from active party politics and retreated to spend more time at Dalmeny.

There he spent much time writing, including a biography of his old friend Sir Randolph Churchill, father of Sir Winston.

To find peace for his work Lord Rosebery deserted the bustle of the big house and walked across the lawns to the shores of the Forth where he sought the seclusion of the oldest building on the estate — the miniature castle of Barnbougle.

Rosebery was particularly proud of twelfth century Barnbougle as he was responsible in 1880 for its complete restoration.

One story, which could well have featured in the pages of the books which lined its walls, was that of the castle itself, for, according to legend, it was haunted by a most unusual ghost.

Local tradition has it that Barnbougle originally belonged to a noble family called Mowbray, whose most famous member, Sir Roger, was a member of the Knights of St John, who had their Scottish headquarters ten miles away at Torphichen Preceptory in the Bathgate Hills.

The knights were famed for the part they played in the Crusades against the Moslem Saracens, and the time came for Sir Roger to travel to the Middle East to join the fray.

When departure day dawned, Sir Roger rose early and made his own brief pilgrimage to the little Norman church which stands to this day in Dalmeny village. There he knelt in prayer. His devotions over, he returned to his castle down by the river and made his way out to the rocky point beneath Barnbougle, where a small sailing ship awaited him.

Just as it cast off, the large hound, which always accompanied Sir Roger when he went hunting, came bounding down the rocks and leapt aboard. The knight did not have the heart to put his faithful dog ashore and so it accompanied him to the Holy Land.

In Palestine, Sir Roger was killed in batle. What became of his hound is not recorded, but it is said that on dark winter nights, when winds whip up the waves on the shore below Barnbougle, its mournful howls can still be heard as it hunts for its long-lost master.

To this day the rocky promontory is called Hound Point.

The Liberal statesman never appears to have been troubled by the ghostly dog, his thoughts, perhaps, being more on his famous stable of racehorses which three times won the Derby — in 1894, 1895 and 1905.

Lord Rosebery's other great interest during his retirement at Dalmeny was his estate and while it is only now that his mansion house is to be opened to the public, the grounds have for many years been opened on Sundays in March to allow visitors to admire the acres of snowdrops which provide Mons Hill with a white carpet.

Dalmeny is now the site for the storeage tanks for the processed north sea oil waiting to be exported via the 100,000 ton tankers which put in at British Petroleum's man made island situated just down river from the Railway Bridge.

As far as Dalmeny is concerned, however, the arrival of the oil industry would not really be anything new, because exactly a century ago it found itself caught up in Scotland's first oil bonanza, which at the time caused as much excitement as the discovery of North Sea oil is creating today.

Dalmeny's earlier experience of life as an oil boom village occurred when James "Pariffin" Young discovered the oil-bearing properties of shale, and rich seams of this oily brown mineral were discovered in the area.

Miners were soon at work beneath the fields around the village, while one of the shale mines ran all the way out beneath the bed of the River Forth. Ancillary industries, including a large brickworks, sprang up, but the discovery of more lucrative sources of oil in the Middle East and America brought Dalmeny's oil industry to an end.

Now the only reminder of it is the bing of red shale ash, much of which was used to provide a base for the approach roads to the Forth Road Bridge.

Apart from this brief flurry of industrial activity during Victorian times, Dalmeny's story has always been a rural one. With its tree-lined village green and its squat, square-towered Norman church, this village has a definitely English look about it.

Dalmeny Church is dedicated to St Cuthbert, as is Durham Cathedral, and from the many masons' marks to be found at Dalmeny it seems almost certain that the same master craftsmen who built the great North of England church also built this little church in West Lothian.

Just what fine craftsmen these itinerant masons were can be judged at Dalmeny from the intricately carved arch stones over the south door, which depict a veritable menagerie of animals.

There are also several stones depicting people, including one of a king seated on a throne, before which a knight is paying homage.

In contrast to the intricacies of this exterior archway, the inside of Dalmeny Parish Church is marked by its simplicity. Here it was that Sir Roger Mowbray is said to have sought God's blessing before he set out on his ill-fated Crusade, and in modern times, too, the peace and quite of this little church have been appreciated by men who have been forced to fight, a fact remembered by the stained-glass in the windows of the apse, which was gifted to the church by the Polish Army officers who were stationed in the area during the last war.

Dalmeny Church

The only part of Dalmeny Church which is not exactly as it was built in the twelfth century is the tower, which was reconstructed in 1926 and which has been criticised ever since for being out of proportion. Perhaps if the oil industry does now come to Dalmeny one of the wealthy oil firms may see fit to donate money to remodel the tower, thus perfecting this the finest of Scotland's Norman churches.

Chapter 12

Into Fife

Midway between Inverkeithing and Aberdour, on the Fife coast of the Firth of Forth, Dalgety, Scotland's latest new town, is swiftly beginning to take shape.

It is still less than twenty years since work began on Dalgety, the site for Scotland's first privately-built new town, but the history of this beautiful spot, set high above the Forth looking out towards Edinburgh, dates back over six hundred years. According to local tradition, Dalgety's first inhabitants came from Denmark, from where they had fled because of religious persecution.

This origin may help to explain some of the comments of the Rev. Alexander Watt in his description of the village in 1836 in the *New Statistical Account of Scotland.* Mr Watt, who was Dalgety's parish minister, stated that the village was a very self-contained little community, with customs and traditions all its own. Most important of these was the active discouragement of any of the village's young people from marrying anyone from beyond its boundaries. Because of this, the same surnames (Dalgety itself was one) were preserved from generation to generation.

Another reason for the close-knit nature of Dalgety village life was the fact that its inhabitants earned their living from coal mining, and as in other parts of Scotland in the eighteenth and early nineteenth centuries, miners, because of their dreadful conditions, were treated as a race apart.

The village had a thriving coal-exporting trade with England and the Low Countries of Europe. Indeed, according to the *New Statistical Account,* coal from Dalgety was well known all over Europe for its superior quality which, it was believed, made it especially suitable for the new wonder of the age—"steam navigation".

The ruins of the old church contrast with these modern homes in the new town of Dalgety Bay.

Dalgety's situation on the shores of the Forth meant that cargoes of coal could be shipped direct, thus avoiding a long and difficult journey overland in days when Scotland's roads left much to be desired and railways had not yet been built. One of the earliest forerunners of a proper railway in Scotland was, in fact, the wooden track laid to link Dalgety's colliery at Fordel with the village harbour at St David's.

From early morning until late at night, six days a week, the horsedrawn waggons, each carrying three tons of coal, trundled up and down the little track. The rails were made of two layers of wood, one of fir and one of beech, with sleepers every two feet.

When they reached the quayside the loads were tipped straight into the little sailing ships which lay waiting to take the coal down the Forth to London or Holland. For a time during the 1830's, cargoes from Dalgety were even shipped all the way to America.

Only the best coal was exported, but the dross was not wasted. Some of the small coal was sold to the bakers and brewers of Dunfermline, but most of it was used in Dalgety itself by the village's other industry, salt-making. Large quantities were always required to keep the fires burning day and night beneath the big pans in which the sea water was evaporated, leaving behind the fine, white crystals of salt that made up another valuable export.

Originally it was the task of the women and children of Dalgety to work the huge wooden pump used to raise the water from the river, but at the beginning of the nineteenth century this back-breaking job was taken over by one of the new steam engines, which were at that time making possible the Industrial Revolution.

This ever-increasing use of steam power meant a corresponding increase in the demand for coal, and in order to increase the export of coal from Dalgety, the local landowner and owner of Fordel Colliery, Admiral Sir Philip Durham, decided to improve the village harbour suitable for vessels of up to 500 tons. Unfortunately, his enterprise was not rewarded, for he had reckoned without the coming of the railways which ended Dalgety's advantage of transporting coal by sea.

Thus, despite Sir Philip's efforts Dalgety's export of coal swiftly declined, and soon the village suffered a second blow when the demand for salt also dwindled due to the opening of salt mines in both England and Europe.

On the land, too, changes were taking place at Dalgety, with the

introduction of the hated enclosure system of agriculture—hated, because it robbed many farm labourers of their livelihood and resulted in the demolition of many cottages to make way for the new fields.

Even the village school was knocked down, but so determined were the remaining villagers that their children should be educated that they opened their own private school in a house down at the foot of the hill near the harbour. For every subject which their sons and daughters were taught they paid fees to pay for the upkeep of the building and to provide the dominie with a salary, which they proudly claimed, was as large as that received by any other schoolmaster in the whole of Fife.

Now, a century later, a fine new primary school has been built for the children of Dalgety's new inhabitants, whose modern villas and bungalows look out at the magnificent view which attracted the fugitive Danes so many years ago. Most of the "newcomers" commute each day back and forth across the Forth Road Bridge to work in Edinburgh, but gradually a feeling of community spirit is coming into being.

The new inhabitants of Dalgety have been left a high standard to aim at by their nineteenth century predecessors, who were described by their parish minister in the *New Statistical Account* as "the most sober, and civilised of their class anywhere to be found".

An extract from one of Andrew Carnegie's speeches reads—"One of my earliest recollections is that of being wakened in the darkness to be told that my Uncle Morrison was in jail. Well, it is one of the proudest boasts I can make today to be able to say that I had an uncle who was in jail. For, ladies and gentlemen, my uncle went to jail to vindicate the rights of public meeting".

Dunfermline's famous benefactor made the speech when he opened the town's new technical college in October 1899, and it is one of the few reminders today of the Chartists and of their fiercely fought campaign — which brought the Army out in Fife.

The Chartists took their name from the People's Charter, a six-point document which demanded the vote for every man; voting by secret ballot; equal voting areas; payment of MPs; the abolition of the need to own property before a man could become an MP; and annual parliamentary elections.

The Government arrested the national leaders of the movement, Feargus O'Connor and Willaim Lovett, but in 1842 they were released and this was the sign for a great upsurge of support.

And nowhere in Scotland was this support more so than in Fife, where feelings among the working people were already running high because of the tremendous amount of unemployment caused by the collapse of the linen industry, and the huge increase in the cost of living due to soaring bread prices caused by the hated Corn Laws.

In Fife, the Chartists' leader was Carnegie's uncle, Thomas Morrison, and he supported the popular demand for a day holiday to enable all the workers to meet to discuss their problems and how the Charter could help to right them.

But, from the outset, he made it clear that he was completely opposed to the kind of violent rioting which had recently taken place in Dunfermline.

This was, in fact the main point which he made at a mass meeting of all the miners and weavers from as far apart as Carnock to Cowdenbeath who gathered in Dunfermline to declare a week's strike in favour of the Charter.

Addressing the crowd of more than 20,000 workers, he stressed that while he would lead them in their struggle to get Parliament to pass the demands set out in the Charter, he would not tolerate the use of any physical force.

He told them that he had in fact, himself enlisted as a special constable to help ensure that there was no violence.

At meetings in Crossgates and the other small Fife industrial villages, Morrison succeeded in holding the crowds by his oratory, and no damage of any kind occurred.

But, the authorities refused to believe that he could manage to maintain this situation at the climax to the whole week's campaign — a mass meeting at Torryburn Ness overlooking the River Forth. So, they called out the Army.

On the morning of the big meeting, bands paraded back and forth through the streets of Dunfermline to summon the strikers for the march to Torryburn.

Before setting out, Morrison again stressed that they were not even "to pull an ear of wheat or even a leaf from a hedge," and that stewards had been appointed to ensure they kept to the middle of the road.

Still, the authorities were not impressed, and before the strikers left, the Sheriff of Fife set out at the head of two contingents of soldiers from the Enniskillen Dragoons and the Forty Second Regiment.

With banners waving the crowd marched peacefully to Torryburn, but no sooner did Morrison start his speech, than the Sherriff appeared with the Procurator-Fiscal and announced that the meeting was illegal — and if all those present did not disperse without delay then the troops would be used.

Morrison was prepared for this and ordered his followers to march with him across the county boundary into what then was part of Perthshire, where the Sheriff had no jurisdiction.

At the boundary the strikers marched over a small bridge. It was this that Morrison took as a symbol when he made his speech in a field on the other side.

"I would have the Sheriff, and I would have you, to understand that whatever may be the efforts made to put down public meetings and free discussions, yet let the people keep within the law, and there always will be a bridge for them to march over."

But, on this occasion, it was the Sheriff who had the last word. For immediately Morrison returned into Fife he was arrested and charged "with forming an illegal conspiracy," and spent more than forty days in jail.

In the end, though, over a period of many years, one by one the Chartists demands were all accepted, apart from their idea of annual elections, although the maximum life of any government was reduced from seven to the present five.